The Adventure
of Reason

Recent Titles in Contributions in Sociology
Series Editor: Don Martindale

The Adventure of Reason

The Uses of
Philosophy in Sociology

H. P. Rickman

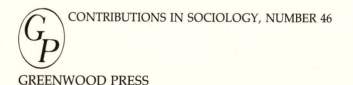

CONTRIBUTIONS IN SOCIOLOGY, NUMBER 46

GREENWOOD PRESS

WESTPORT, CONNECTICUT • LONDON, ENGLAND

100082

Copyright Acknowledgments

Grateful acknowledgment is given for permission to use the following:

Extracts from *Discourse on Method* by Réné Descartes, translated by Arthur Wollaston, Harmondsworth: Penguin Classic Series, 1960. Reprinted by permission of Penguin Books Ltd.

Extracts from *Republic* by Plato, translated by Desmond Lee. Harmondsworth: Penguin Classic Series, 1955. Reprinted by permission of Penguin Books Ltd.

Library of Congress Cataloging in Publication Data

Rickman, H. P. (Hans Peter)
   The adventure of reason.

   (Contributions in sociology, ISSN 0084-9278; no. 46)
   Bibliography: p.
   Includes index.
   1. Sociology—Philosophy. 2. Reason—Philosophy.
I. Title. II. Series.
HM24.R4863 1983   301'.01   83-5622
ISBN 0-313-23871-5 (lib. bdg.)

Library of Congress Catalog Card Number: 83-5622
ISBN: 0-313-23871-5
ISSN: 0084-9278

First published in 1983

Greenwood Press
A division of Congressional Information Service, Inc.
88 Post Road West
Westport, Connecticut 06881

Printed in the United States of America

10 9 8 7 6 5 4 3 2 1

HM
585
.R45
1983

In memory of my wife
Among her gifts to me was help with all my writing.

Contents

Preface

The aim of this book is to introduce sociologists and indeed
anyone interested in the life of society to some philosophic ideas.
It is based on the belief that the study of society—like any other
search for knowledge—involves broad assumptions and the use
of concepts and methods which can be illuminated by reference
to philosophy.

Such an approach must be severely selective for a work which
tries to pay even lip service to the wealth and variety of philosophic ideas, and the many thinkers who contributed to a continuous debate can too easily degenerate into lists and labels.
For this reason I have chosen a single theme—the role of reason.
As important to our whole intellectual tradition as to philosophy
itself, the role of reason has a relevance to sociology which has
been insufficiently explored. To make this study manageable I
had to limit myself further to four thinkers who signpost the
development of this theme up to the point when sociology developed into an independent discipline in the beginning of the
nineteenth century. Once philosophy acquired the new function
of entering into a dialogue with that new science, the approach
changed, requiring separate treatment. For this reason I have
concentrated on the earlier period when concepts vital to the
eventual development of sociology, such as causality, function,
role, purpose, and types were forged, and fundamental methods
of inquiry developed.

The choice of Plato, Descartes, Spinoza, and Kant requires

little justification, for they are indisputably four of the most important philosophers in Western thought. They all contributed incisively to the tradition of reason and thereby to the armoury of concepts and methods which sociology came to use with profit.

The choice of Plato is the most obvious. He is the first systematic philosopher of the West, or at least the first whose writings have been passed on to us. What is more, after two and a half thousand years of philosophy, he still towers over all his successors. He also made ingenious beginnings in the practice of sociology and contributed to social theory. His tremendous shadow falls over sociology as it does over the whole of our civilisation.

If Plato can be described as the father of Western philosophy, Descartes can be called the father of modern philosophy. He ushered in a new age of thought by focussing attention on the theory of knowledge and by suggesting and prophetically anticipating the development of science and technology which was to transform our world. His chief relevance to sociology lies in his critical reflections on methods.

Spinoza was one of the greatest metaphysicians, and no one has spelled out a rational system of philosophy more concisely and cogently than he did. Not only did he give the clearest and most incisive account of the presuppositions on which rationality must rest, but he also expounded and made intellectually respectable a cognitive approach which was to prove tremendously important for all the human studies.

In Kant, whose thinking was decisive in the history of philosophy, the theory of knowledge reached its peak of sophistication. Philosophy had lost its innocence. Nothing in the intellectual life of the West could be the same again once Kant had completed his devastating analyses. His influence on moral philosophy was equally important, for no one before him had worked out the moral implication of the autonomy of reason with equal profundity.

Although each of these four thinkers had specific things to say about social life, and Plato in particular is a mine of sociological thought, it would trivialise their contribution to sociological thought if one concentrated entirely on these aspects of their work. It is their purely philosophical reflections which in the long run proved influential for all our thinking and laid the foundations for understanding the social world. I have therefore tried to deal systematically with some of their central arguments, and to help the reader I have concentrated in each case on one or two important and easily available texts. Plato is represented by *The Republic*, Descartes by *The Discourse on Method* and *The Meditations* (usually available in one volume), Spinoza by *The Ethic*, and Kant by *The Critique of Pure Reason* and *The Groundwork of the Metaphysic of Morals*. This does not exclude, of course, cross-references to other of their works or to the writing of sociologists and philosophers of the social sciences.

The first chapter explains in what way philosophy can be of use to sociology. The next chapters deal with the four philosophers in turn, starting with a brief account of their lives, personalities, and works and continuing to an exposition of their main thoughts and a discussion of their relevance for sociology. The final chapter relates the main philosophic themes to major issues of contemporary sociology. The selected bibliography includes books quoted in the text and listed in notes sections and suggests further reading in the philosophy of the social sciences.

*The Adventure
of Reason*

1 . *Sociology and Philosophy*

This book is written in the belief that students of society may find it useful to learn about the thoughts of philosophers who have taken reason for their theme. Because any systematic study of society must be guided by reason, the choice of theme needs little justification, but the insistence that it should be philosophically treated does. One may naturally ask why people engaged in the down-to-earth search for factual knowledge and practical understanding should have thrust upon their notice such philosophic activities as speculating about fundamental ideas, analysing concepts, examining basic assumptions, and drawing up intellectual maps. What need is there for observers engrossed in the pageantry of human life to chase abstract ideas?

To show that philosophy, besides being enjoyable and absorbing, can be of direct use in the study of society one needs to argue, firstly, that all systematic research rests on a framework of very general presuppositions, and, secondly, that in the case of sociology that framework cannot be taken for granted.

Coming to know something is not just a matter of allowing reality to impress itself on our minds. The messages which reach us become knowledge only when they fit into a whole context of ideas and presuppositions about the capacities of our minds and the nature of our subject matter. We could not, for example, account for any knowledge without presupposing a power of reason in ourselves and some principles of order, such as causality in nature. Knowledge about the human world involves

additional assumptions about man and society. That man is purposive, capable of reason, and dependent on a web of social
relationships are not things we merely discover in the course of
investigations, but assumptions we bring to them. Other assumptions concern the relationship between body and mind or
the degree of flexibility in human nature.

The kinds of assumptions we make on these matters are important, because they influence personal conduct, education,
and politics; most relevant for our purpose, they determine how
we conduct research. Because of their importance these assumptions need to be clarified, critically examined, and occasionally revised. This is a job very different from what sociologists
normally do, but the normal preoccupation of philosophers. Far
from being just a game played for its own sake or one which
makes sense only when science cannot yet replace guesses and
anticipations with solid knowledge, this concern with basic assumptions has a serious and abiding function. By examining or
even creating general assumptions about the world, philosophy
projects overall pictures of what we want to study and sets out
criteria for what can count as knowledge. Both are indispensable
in the practical pursuit of knowledge, for without such guidance
we would not be able to distinguish alchemy from chemistry or
old wives' tales from sociology. We would be too sceptical to
initiate research or, as happens more frequently, too credulous
to achieve objective results. Furthermore, history testifies that
intelligent and well-educated people believed in possession by
the devil and in black magic until their frame of reference was
shattered by a new philosophical theory of knowledge (that of
Descartes).[1] What we accept as true and scientifically sound and
what we condemn as prejudice or superstition, what we praise
as common sense or decry as madness, depends on the philosophic framework we have come to accept.

But even so, why should students of the social world actually
study the philosophical arguments by which their presuppositions are developed and secured? Why can they not, once the
job is done, enjoy its results without further worry? After all,
neither in everyday life nor in the physical sciences do we feel
the need to go constantly back to the basic presuppositions of
our thinking. For the physicist, for example, the history of sci-

ence may be interesting and stimulating but not essential to his work.

Four outstanding reasons may be given to explain why sociology needs to go back to first principles. Sociology must justify the increasingly important role it plays in social life; it must satisfy or discourage some very high expectations of what it can acccomplish; it must confront problems about objectivity which are inherent in the subject matter; and for these reasons it remains divided about its methods.

The increasingly important role sociology plays in modern life, both its popularity and its expansion, is largely a response to the growing complexity of modern life. People living in modern mass society, not in small, relatively self-contained communities, do not know as neighbours or friends the political leaders, officials, traders, and others with whom they have to deal and have not learned from experience how to treat them. Because people function as members of bureaucracies, political parties, or trade unions or as employees of supermarkets, nationalised industries, or insurance companies, they can be understood only in terms of the way these organisations work and influence the behaviour of their members. Even understanding people in personal relationships may require knowing about social backgrounds unfamiliar to us. Thus the practical need arises for such disciplines as sociology which study these social contexts and offer guidance about behaviour between employer and employee, parent and child, husband and wife.

By assuming such responsibilities sociology becomes controversial. While some people eagerly seek sociological help with town planning, industrial relations, or education, others resent such interference. Where sociology lays bare the working of social institutions it is accused of subversive criticism; where it teaches how to smooth the functioning of social organisations it is suspected of being a lackey of the existing order. Forced to deal with morally sensitive issues, the sociologist is propelled into the arena of social and political controversy.

The expectations aroused by sociology extend beyond its role of analysing social relationships and recommending techniques of coping with them. A widespread decline in religious faith and a growing scepticism about philosophically based world views have made people turn for comprehension and guidance to the most highly respected part of our culture, to science. While obviously commenting on human life, sociology appeals to the scientific temper of our age by relying on empirical evidence and careful inference rather than on faith and speculation. The student of the human world, it is felt, must have something worth saying about human destiny, about the faults and follies of social arrangements, and about the direction human efforts should take. The mantle of guide and prophet falls on his more or less willing shoulders.

The problem of objectivity raised by the role required of sociology and the expectations aroused by it, has deeper roots. For good or ill we know social life intimately from within, because we are not only involved in social relations from birth but create them by our own feelings and attitudes. This personal stake gives us privileged insights but often makes the subject painful or embarrassing. Observing attitudes similar to or very different from our own and recognising reactions which may affect us, we may easily be too indulgent or too censorious. Shrinking from studying critically what touches us so closely, we may turn with relief to the less tantalising study of nature. This may be one of the reasons why the physical sciences appear to have advanced further than disciplines concerned with man.

The difficulties and challenges I have listed have helped to perpetuate a fourth problem: the continuing conflict among sociologists themselves about the nature, goals, and methods of their subject. There is no single, agreed-upon paradigm that can be taken for granted.

These different problems force the sociologist to reexamine fundamental issues. Propelled into the political arena, he must demonstrate that his methods protect him from his natural prejudices. Asked to adjudicate on moral and social issues, he can neither absentmindedly ignore nor complacently accept this role but must justify whatever view of sociology he takes in terms of a critical evaluation of its scope and methods. The danger of personal bias, too, forces him to become methodologically self-conscious. The continued debates within sociology offer the same lesson, the need for a critical examination of the presuppositions on which sociology rests.

The issues thus raised are the traditional subject matter of philosophy. The apparent paradox that what concerns the sociologist is the philosopher's subject uncovers the underlying unity within intellectual life, which is hidden by the need for more and more specialisation precipitated by the growth of knowledge. In this book I have picked from the web of interdependencies the use sociologists can make of philosophy. One could just as readily single out such topics as how knowledge of social contexts or the methodology of the social sciences can throw light on the work of philosophers.

It is important to stress the underlying unity of our intellectual heritage, because we are not simply talking about individual sociologists calling upon—and possibly receiving—the help of their colleagues in philosophy departments. Such interdepartmental cooperation can be useful but is as yet rare. There are probably not enough philosophers of the social sciences; interest in that field has revived only fairly recently and requires a competent knowledge of the social sciences which only a minority of philosophers currently possess.

We are thus concerned with a part of a heritage which we all can share and which in fact has been shared to some extent, for the achievements in one sphere have often been absorbed in another. Though sociology as a separate discipline with its own methodology is only about 150 years old, it is, like other cognitive enterprises, heir to a common intellectual tradition which stretches back over millenia. Concern with social life is a persisting strand in that tradition, and historians, theologians, jurists, economists, political theoreticians, poets, dramatists, and, last but not least, philosophers have been engaged in recording social behaviour and theorising about it long before the separate existence of sociology. This tradition also forged the basic concepts, assumptions, and attitudes which lie at the base of all disciplined inquiry. Here philosophy, from its beginnings in Greece some 2,600 years ago, has played an outstanding part.

By relating highlights from the history of philosophy to fundamental issues of sociology I want to drive home the point that we are joined in an intellectual adventure and can draw strength from awareness of our common roots and shared problems. If the individual disciplines, be they philosophy, sociology, or any other, are content to play in their own corners, they condemn themselves to sterility.

The adventure I am talking about is the pursuit of knowledge, the effort to ground and justify by reason what we believe to be true. The transition from superstition and blind belief to knowledge, from hit and miss, trial and error, to systematic research comes with the application of rational criteria. The resolve to submit one area of life after another to such critical questioning I call—using a phrase of Kant's—'the adventure of reason'. Sociology is part of this adventure, as is any discipline which seeks truth based on proper evidence. Historians join this great tradition when they cease to accept past records and travellers' tales unquestioningly; scientists, when they put theories to rigorous tests; moralists, when they question why particular rules, sanctioned by tradition, should be obeyed; and sociologists, when they try to translate into systematic knowledge our everyday guesses and groping attempts to understand the social world. It is, however, philosophy which is most explicitly and systematically committed to this adventure. Every philosophic work is intended as an exercise in critical reason and is thus a contribution to the adventure of reason. Or if one prefers, each is a separate adventure in the exercise of reason.

All philosophy is committed to the use of reason as its prime instrument, even if, like all human activities, it sometimes fails in its aims. The subject matter of philosophy is a wide range of topics such as experience, art, morality, and politics. Nevertheless philosophical reflection on reason itself and on the application of rational principles to this varied subject matter is a central thread within philosophy, which I call the philosophy of reason. Having a wider meaning than such labels as "rationalism," the philosophy of reason describes a persistent theme within philosophy rather than a particular school of philosophy. This central tradition has a very special bearing on the intellectual challenges which confront sociology, as becomes clear when we explain its nature.

The Philosophy of Reason

Characterising philosophic tradition in a few words can do justice neither to its richness nor to the uniqueness of individual contributions. Nonetheless we can identify some crucial features which justify our attaching a common label to the work of many generations of thinkers. By selecting and explaining four of its crucial principles, it is possible to give an idea of what the philosophy of reason stands for. Not that all philosophers of reason have been equally clear and explicit about these fundamental principles: the development of one principle after another is itself part of the history of this philosophic movement. But these four principles form the hard core of the philosophy of reason. The first is that we should only accept as true what is based on sound, critically examined evidence and valid reasoning; the second is that reality is knowable because it has a rational and therefore rationally intelligible structure; the third stresses the importance of self-knowledge; and the last concerns man's power to direct his actions rationally not only in the selection of means but also in the choice of ends. Even this short summary may give students of sociology an idea of the relevance of these principles to their subject.

The idea that we must accept only what is based on sound, critically examined evidence was first, and most incisively, formulated in Plato's *Apology*. Five centuries before Christ, Plato describes how Socrates defended himself against the charges of impiety and corrupting the young of Athens. It marked a turning point in man's intellectual history, for Socrates claimed that all traditional wisdom, religious revelation, myths, legends, and oracular pronouncements must be subjected to rational inquiry before they can be accepted. After telling his judges that the Delphic oracle had pronounced him the wisest of all men, a judgement which he—though a believer in the truthfulness of God and the authenticity of the oracle—found puzzling, he continued: 'After a long consideration I thought of a method of trying the question. I reflected that if I could only find a man wiser than myself, then I might go to the God with a refutation in my hand. I should say to him, "Here is a man who is wiser than I am; but you said I was wisest".'[2]

Here, with breathtaking confidence and unprecedented clarity, the voice of reason is calling for a critical use of experience to establish the truth. We see Socrates applying in the fifth century B.C. the kind of rational test K. R. Popper has singled out in our own time as the central feature of the scientific method.[3] What is more, Socrates applies it to a divine pronouncement, treating it as a hypothesis to be tested by attempts to refute it. Socrates' concern with questions about how we can gain reliable knowledge—of which the above is only one, though an outstanding, example—was but a beginning. Those questions have continued to occupy philosophers to this day.

The second principle, that reality, to be knowable, must have a rational structure, though first adumbrated in ancient Greek philosophy, was spelled out by seventeenth-century rationalists like Spinoza and developed most explicitly by the idealists of the nineteenth century, Hegel foremost among them. Kant, whose work falls into the period between Spinoza and Hegel, espoused a modified and attenuated version of this principle, and so did the neo-Kantians of the late nineteenth century. In modern philosophy the confidence in a correspondence between the principles which guide cognition and those which govern reality has been eroded if not eclipsed. In science too the conviction that our theoretical schemes actually correspond to the ultimate nature of reality has progressively declined. We have become more sceptical; the truth seems elusive, the journey towards it infinitely long. Yet something of the second principle remains as a necessary presupposition of the scientist's work. Whatever role conventions, hypothetical constructions, and fictional entities may play in science, they cannot wholly account for its conclusions, or there would never be a reason for changing or retaining a theory. It does not make sense to extrapolate generalisations from experience, to formulate laws and anticipate that the regularities established today will be part of tomorrow's world, unless reality does contain something of the order we attribute to it, and we can rely on nature's being subject to laws which we can comprehend. However suspicious modern science has become about its own capacity to look into the ultimate nature of things, it cannot wholly abandon its belief in an intelligible reality without losing faith in its own results.

The third principle, which insists on the importance of self-knowledge, is an extension of the first principle. If everything must be examined rationally, the mind must turn its critical scrutiny even upon its own activities. This stress on self-knowledge was part of the original awakening of rational inquiry in ancient Greece. In the further development of philosophy, particularly since the seventeenth century, a more subtle link between the first and third principles has been recognized. It is argued that to examine the foundations of knowledge inevitably involves self-knowledge, because what is at issue is a critical scrutiny of the mind's cognitive powers. This scrutiny, called epistemology or theory of knowledge, has become one of the main preoccupations of philosophy since Descartes.

Finally, the fourth principle stipulates that reason can be practical, can guide action by providing moral principles, as well as prudential considerations, which can be rationally discussed. This principle is absolutely central to the philosophy of reason, because it gives reason the moral authority with which the first and third principles are able to call for particular actions or attitudes. To be credulous and neglect your reason is not only dangerous to your safety and comfort; it is wrong, because it conflicts with human dignity. Not to seek self-knowledge is despicable and a betrayal of man's true nature: better to be Socrates dissatisfied than a pig satisfied.[4] If we could not claim a rational basis for these moral judgements, the whole philosophy of reason would depend on an irrational factor. The autonomy of reason is only assured by the interdependence of theoretical and practical principles.

So the philosophy of reason is committed to the view that reason, far from confining itself to the task of selecting means to ends, which no one would deny it, can and must provide final goals and fundamental principles. As the source of values it must value itself highly. Exercising reason is not only potentially useful and even enriching but intrinsically worthwhile. Man owes it to himself to think, to know himself, and to direct his actions rationally, for only so does he achieve the highest human state.

Sociology as an Adventure of Reason

Because it is part of the adventure of reason, one aspect among others of man's continued exercise of curiosity and effort to replace ignorance by knowledge and credulity by critical judgement, sociology is indebted to the philosophy of reason. Thus establishing the claims and functions, the scope and limitations of reason is not only crucial within philosophy itself but has played an important part in shaping ideas which were to assume sociological significance.

However, other aspects of philosophy have more often attracted the attention of historians of sociology. Empiricism (and such modern forms of it as positivism) is most frequently claimed to be the basis of the sociologist's outlook, because its clear insistence on experience as the sole source of knowledge appears to be most directly relevant to the construction of an empirical discipline. Exposed to accusations that sociology is a woolly subject, its exponents are sensitive about being scientific and so look to a tradition which is hard-headed and down-to-earth. It should be recalled that Auguste Comte, who invented the term 'sociology,' also proclaimed a positivist philosophy.[5]

Attention to the empirical tradition has proved valuable, because it justifies and encourages careful observation, patient collection of data, and rigorous techniques of evaluating evidence. However, exclusive concentration on the physically observable, the hallmark of empiricism, does less than justice to what most sociologists actually investigate. They are also concerned with such phenomena as loyalty, values, tradition, social cohesion, authority, and religious faith, which are not 'hard' facts easily expressible in behavioural terms. These phenomena were emphasised and systematically examined by a nineteenth-century intellectual movement usually described as Romanticism. Writers on sociology have drawn attention to this fact and showed the Romantic tradition helped to crystallise and clarify concepts and assumptions relevant to sociology, thus proving a useful corrective to empiricism and a stimulus to sociological practice.[6]

Fruitful concern with these philosophic movements has tended to eclipse interest in the philosophy of reason. Yet the philosophy of reason is the source of ideas of very special interest to sociologists and provides the principles on which the methods of sociology must be shown to be based if it is to qualify as a systematic and rigorous discipline. Sociology is nothing if not 'scientific' in the sense that it uses stringent, critically examined methods, tests its theories by solid evidence, and presents its conclusions in a well-defined terminology. It goes without saying that all this includes respect for experience; but a heap of impressions is not science. They must be sifted, examined critically, assessed, and given their place in a system. Indeed experience itself is something more complex and ambiguous than empiricism usually allows. The sociologist's insistence on the critical evaluation of experience and on analysis of what is involved in experiencing derives specifically from the philosophy of reason.

The philosophical clarification of these abstract issues about the nature of knowledge has a direct bearing on certain methodological issues within sociology which, in the absence of a general consensus about the legitimacy and fruitfulness of various approaches, are still hotly debated. Differences ranging from the painstaking observation and statistical analysis of behaviour to the imaginative interpretation of cultural phenomena, from the close study of small groups to literary research designed to decipher the features of a whole civilisation, are more than a sensible division of labour because the practitioners of these different approaches are often sceptical of each other's methods. This diversity suggests the value of a return to fundamentals, a philosophical reappraisal fo the cognitive approaches which are possible and fruitful in the human sphere.

Part of the debt which the methodology of sociology owes to the philosophy of reason, it shares with other disciplines, because they are all concerned with the pursuit of truth. However, other ideas generated by the philosophy of reason, such as those of teleology and system, are of specific value to sociology, because they suggest or justify lines of approach particularly suitable for the study of society. Beside this there is a further, unique link between the philosophy of reason and sociology: the latter has reason and its products for its subject matter. Man himself, as he appears in the sociologist's perspectives, is a rational being— clearly not always, perhaps only occasionally rational, but capable of reason nevertheless and using this capacity in decisive ways. It has enabled him to create complex, highly organised societies which contain and depend on laws, moral codes, institutions, organisations, and an accumulation of knowledge. All these manifestations, which bear the stamp of reason, are part of the sociologist's subject matter.

This does not mean that the social world as a whole, or even any of its parts, is rationally planned. People are not motivated only by reason, but also by passions and prejudices. The clash of interests between individuals or groups produces results which no one planned. The same is true of the uncoordinated activities of individuals. Yet there are rational structures which we can trace. Human beings can be swayed by good reasons and tangible evidence; they can work out the best means for their chosen ends. All this the investigator can follow, and even when people act in a foolhardy way their behaviour can be understood in terms of a deviation from a rational norm. (If he had been rational, he would have taken a plane to reach his goal on time. Why didn't he?)

Today most people are not convinced that the universe as a whole is rational, because they believe neither that the world is designed and run by a rational God nor that it is produced by an abstract, rational principle. But what, in the case of nature as a whole, is at best a sustaining hypothesis, is in the human world a fact. The researcher can rightly assume that his subject has as much rationality, and of the same kind, as he does. This gives the social scientist an advantage not enjoyed by the physicist or chemist, who must deal with unthinking matter.

As well as preparing the ground for the methods of sociology and analysing a crucial aspect of its subject matter, the philosophy of reason also provides the sociologist with the moral aim and justification he needs to meet the challenges confronting him. Sociology serves man's self-knowledge and so responds to the imperative spelled out in the philosophy of reason. By coming to understand how society functions, mankind comes to understand itself better, and even individual men deepen their self-awareness by realising how far and in what way they are social beings shaped by social forces to the very core. Seen in this light, sociology is not just idle curiosity, and the sociologist not just a peeping Tom and indefatigable meddler in others' affairs. He contributes to the collective self-understanding which makes us more truly human.

There is a further twist in the relevance of this moral imperative to sociology. The imperative reminds the sociologist that he is dealing with creatures who have a capacity for, and a duty towards, self-knowledge. In empirical fact they often seek such knowledge, though not always genuinely. It is thus character- istic of his subject and affects his methodology that the objects of his study have views about themselves. In his own effort towards knowledge he must take into account, though he need not necessarily accept, what is claimed to be the self-knowledge of others. Where he challenges such self-knowledge, or increases or modifies it, he assumes a special moral responsibility of which he should be aware.

The relationship between sociology and the fourth principle of the philosophy of reason, that reason is an ultimate basis for action, is more complex and particularly interesting. Sociology interests itself in human actions and therefore in their motives, among which it discovers ideals and moral principles, or, to put it more cautiously, the claims of people to be motivated by them. These claims, those made sincerely and those more or less ob- viously hypocritical, play an active part in social life. Whether we agree or disagree with the philosophy of reason about the possibility of making objective moral statements, we cannot deny that assertions that some things are right and others wrong are actually put forward with the conviction that they are objectively justified and not just someone's opinion. If this were not so, it would be impossible to understand why people should pay even hypocritical lip service to morality. This claim to objectivity must therefore be taken seriously. Even if morality were invariably a mask for self- or class-interests, the lineaments of that mask would still merit careful examination. The philosophy of reason provides a basis for this examination because it presents rea- soned arguments which try to make sense of the claim to ob- jectivity which morality—as a matter of fact—invariably makes.

Morality raises a second, critical issue, namely that of freedom. Sociology must try to account for human actions in terms of social determinants. Pushed to its extremes this implies that what people do is predetermined: they could never have done anything else. Biological inheritance and environment impose severe limitations on what we can and cannot do. Socialisation forecloses the remaining options. If we are to explain a person's attitude by, let us say, his working-class origins we are logically compelled to believe that given those origins (and all other things being equal) he could not but hold those attitudes. Yet somehow this distorts the picture of social life. We do not quite recognise as human those actions which do not allow for choice. I can weigh arguments in my own mind or argue with others and assume that whatever their social background, they may 'listen to reason'. The philosophy of reason, in trying to explain how reason can be both autonomous and practical, makes sense of this possibility.

The idea of an objective, because rationally based, morality bestows a further benefit on the sociologist. If he and his audience accept the opposite assumption, namely that morality is relative and socially determined, he finds himself in a predicament to which I have already alluded. He cannot, however hard he tries, be entirely neutral about moral issues.[7] When he chooses a subject and decides to investigate particular features of a situation, he is already suggesting that the subject is important and that the features he has selected demand more attention than others. He also implies frequently that there is something wrong in the situation which needs putting right. If, for example, someone studies the influence that housing has on delinquency, he probably thinks that delinquency is a serious problem and that there is something wrong with housing which should be put right. Even when the sociologist avoids explicit moral terminology, he uses concepts which, though overtly descriptive, carry a moral meaning. Normal and abnormal, functional and dysfunctional, reification and alienation, are concepts of this kind. They are clearly not neutral, for it would sound paradoxical to say what a good thing it was that something was dysfunctional, or that we ought to make an effort to increase alienation.

If, then, the sociologist maintains that valuations are socially determined but is unable to refrain from valuations himself, he is in an invidious position. He is either seen as sanctifying the existing order or as undermining it by his analysis, as either an instrument of the ruling classes or as a beetle eating away the beams on which society rests. A philosophy like that of reason provides him with an escape from this dilemma, because it suggests that the moral judgements which he studies sociologically can also be judged independently by reason.

The philosophy of reason which has so powerfully affected

the direction of Western thought and provided foundations for the study of society, as for much else, owes many of its outstanding developments to the four thinkers I have chosen to represent it. Between them they spelled out the principles of reason, supported them by powerful arguments, and used them in the construction of their philosophies. In their work the reader will see in a new and illuminating context ideas which he encountered in the study of society. He will then be able to judge for himself how far the philosophic discussion of these ideas help sociology to meet the challenges it faces today.

2 • *Plato: The Rule of Reason*

At the very dawn of European philosophy, Plato put forward the most confident and comprehensive claims ever made on behalf of reason. In a series of philosophical dialogues he spelled out his thesis that a perfect, rational, and intelligible order lies behind the untidy and confusing everyday world we perceive with our senses, and claimed that to know this not only helps us to comprehend the visible world but also provides us with guidelines for personal and political life.

Plato's influence on Europe's intellectual and cultural life has been enormous. To some he is the greatest philosopher of all; Alfred North Whitehead remarked that all subsequent philosophy is a series of footnotes to the Platonic dialogues. Even those who are less enthusiastic would hesitate to exclude him from a list of the five most influential philosophers, for generation after generation has revived his philosophy and reinterpreted it according to the preoccupations of the age. Moreover, his influence is not confined to the development of philosophy; his ideas can be traced in moral attitudes and political theories, in theology and aesthetics, in literature and science, in our views of work, love, and technology.

The richness of Plato's thought has given rise to a vast literature about the interpretation of his subtle arguments, and considerable passion has been aroused by the question whether on balance his influence was beneficial or not. Some think of him as an obstacle who delayed the growth of science; others have hailed him as the prophet of rational inquiry. Some revere him as the great humanist educator who points the way to personal fulfillment; others revile him as the protagonist of a closed and authoritarian society.[1]

From the many-sided and complex body of Plato's theories I have selected a number of central themes relevant to the study of society. One does not have to pick up incidental hints to make out a case for Plato's role in the development of sociological thought. On the contrary, it can be shown that he was profoundly concerned with the understanding of society and that this preoccupation is linked to, and colours, some of his most crucial theories. But it is only fair to remember that in choosing these themes we are merely tracing a few threads in a complex tapestry.

Plato's profound interest in the processes of social change can be accounted for by the conditions of the age in which he lived and the challenge they presented to him. He was born in 427 B.C., the son of an aristocratic family living in Athens when the city was still at the height of its power and dominated the culture of a Greece buoyant with intellectual activity. By the time of his death in 347, the glory of Athens and of Greece was in decline. He had witnessed changes and upheavals which to him spelled social, moral, and political disintegration. Two incidents in particular link his personal life to the turbulence of his time. In 399 his beloved teacher, Socrates, who had previously fallen foul of an oligarchic government, was charged by a democratic one with corrupting young people, tried, condemned, and executed. Socrates' influence had made Plato turn from poetry and politics to philosphy, and he felt obliged to commemorate and continue his master's work. This he did in the bitter conviction that a good and wise man, concerned with the moral regeneration of his country, had been the victim of folly and injustice. The other crucial experience of Plato's life came in 367, when he was invited to supervise the education of the young ruler of Syracuse. He accepted in the hope that by this step he could make philosophical ideas effective in politics, a venture which ended in disillusion and failure.

Plato was a man of profound moral convictions, to which he gave expression in rationally and systematically developed arguments. He was not, however, content to speculate on or judge the views, motives, and actions of his contemporaries but wanted to see his own views translated into action, and society transformed by his ideals. He did not think he could bring this about by direct political action. Perhaps his temperament did not predispose him to such a course; instead, believing that knowledge was essential for successful action, he concentrated his enormous intellectual powers on the question how social changes occurred and how they could be influenced. The many small societies of Greece—the city, states—which changed rapidly and experimented actively with different political institutions provided a rich field for comparative study.

Roles, Functions, and Forms

One of Plato's most famous dialogues, the *Republic*, contains some of the best illustrations of the way in which he forges his intellectual tools for the understanding of society. Of special interest is his development of the concept of social roles which he defined in terms of norms which in turn can only be properly understood by reference to the idea of function. In the hands of a great speculative philosopher these concepts are not ad hoc constructions but related to, and derived from, coherent metaphysical and epistemological theories like that of the Forms, which postulates that the reality corresponding to true knowledge consists of intellectual forms or ideas that provide models which are only imperfectly imitated by the world of our senses.

The theme of the dialogue is justice. As is usual in Plato's work, the subject is raised casually in conversation; then Socrates—here, as in most of the dialogues, the main speaker—pounces. He presses his friends to define justice and shows how confused and uncertain people tend to be about its general concepts.[2] Next Thrasymachus intervenes. He is described with some malice as bumptious and unable to sustain his argument consistently, so that Socrates forces him into a humiliating retreat. However, his theory, apparently one current among bright young men of the time, is of considerable interest. Ever since, various forms of it have cropped up in political theories, of which Marxism is the best known.

'I define justice or right', Thrasymachus claims, 'as what is in the interest of the stronger party.'[3] He goes on to clarify what he means. 'Each ruling class makes laws that are in its own interest . . . and in making these laws defines as "right" for their subjects what is in the interest of themselves, the rulers.[4] This is the hard-headed, positivistic approach to the subject of justice, where any thought of ideals or principles is rejected as highfaluting nonsense: justice is what rulers actually decide on and enforce for ascertainable motives of their own. Throughout the *Republic* this theory is attacked in different ways and on different levels. The underlying conception of social life is challenged and confronted by a different one; the model of society based on conflict resolved through the use of power is replaced by one of cooperation in the fulfillment of different functions.

Socrates' first line of attack is a highly technical one which he uses to argue his way to important insights. Confronted with the assertion that rulers rule in order to serve their own interest, Socrates considers what is involved in talking about the aim of an activity like ruling (or practising medicine, or any other purposive activity), thus raising the whole issue of how individuals are related to the socially defined roles they play in society. Though Plato does not use the term 'role', his discussion covers the topic as defined in modern sociology.

The argument from which the role theory emerges begins with Thrasymachus falling into a logical trap. After his assertion that justice is the interest of the stronger party, he is asked about the case where a ruler is mistaken about his own interests.[5] If, through miscalculation, that ruler promulgates a law which is to his own disadvantage, is such a law just or unjust? Thrasymachus refuses to rephrase his case in terms of what the ruler *thinks* his interest is. Instead he claims that freedom from such mistakes is part of the definition of what it means to be the stronger party. 'Do you,' Thrasymachus asks, 'call a man who has made a mistaken diagnosis a doctor by virtue of his mistake? Or, when a mathematician makes a mistake in his calculations, do you call him a mathematician by virtue of his mistake and when he makes it? We use this form of words, of course, and talk of a doctor, a mathematician or a scholar "making a mistake" but, in fact, I think, each of them, insofar as he is what we call him, is infallible.'[6] He goes on to assert that just as the doctor or scientist is not properly a doctor or a scientist at the moment when his skill fails him, so the ruler is not playing his role when he does not act in his own interest.

Thrasymachus claims to be a hardheaded realist whose views are based solidly on the observation of human behaviour, and when cornered by theoretical arguments, he makes his stand on the facts and accuses Socrates of being unaware that the shepherd looks after sheep in his own interest and the ruler exacts justice 'at the expense of the subject who obeys him'.[7] No doubt, he implies, governments are only too pleased to persuade their subjects that they are performing a service to the community and that their laws enshrine an objective justice which their subjects are under a moral obligation to obey. But this is a pretence, a confidence trick. Those who do not belong to the ruling class are duped if they accept these claims, for their true interest lies in being unjust, in defying or circumventing the rules imposed upon them.[8]

Challenging this selection of facts, which he thinks leads to a rather cynical and one-sided view of human nature and society, Plato points to the need for honour among thieves,[9] suggesting that society is based on the common interests of the governors and the governed.[10] He adds that people who pursue their selfish interests at the expense of others may frustrate their own true interests, describing the loneliness and fear of the tyrant who through his actions has separated himself from fellowship with other people.[11] If, he argues, Thrasymachus' picture were the whole truth, social life and personal fulfillment would be impossible; but he is as realistic as Thrasymachus in recognising the grim realities of selfishness, power struggles, and exploitation of the weak by the strong. In his description of different forms of government, he provides very vivid pictures of the arrogance of military leaders,[12] the exploitation of the poor by the rich,[13] and the enslavement of whole societies by tyrants.[14]

It is important to stress that the disagreement is only marginally about the facts of human behavior, for this helps us to see the real issue more clearly, that is, that Thrasymachus does not realise where his ideas are leading him. He has laid himself open to attack, and is defeated in argument, because he has failed to see the full implications of his own role theory. The infallible ruler or doctor is obviously not a person of flesh and blood whom we can point to and observe. We are talking about roles which people may assume more or less successfully, and a simple appeal to observable facts cannot tell us what it means to be a ruler. Thrasymachus cannot establish the case that justice is the interest of the stronger party simply by pointing to brutal and powerful men exploiting the weak and legislating in their own interest, because according to the argument he has himself put forward, those men may not be acting as rulers when they do those things.

Thrasymachus had intended to show that traditional norms turned out to be hypocritical nonsense when compared with the realities of power politics, but the moment he proposed talking about perfect rulers he had to concede that human behaviour must be interpreted and judged in terms of norms, not norms in terms of human behaviour. So, before we can tell rulers from other people, before we can distinguish ruling from the leisure-time activities of rulers, and, most difficult of all, before we can tell real ruling from fumbling attempts at it, we need a definition of ruling which spells out the norms that determine it. No amount of observation with pencil poised and cameras clicking will help us. No statistical calculations can be illuminating, because it is obvious that rulers may spend more time on hobbies than on their job and, even when working, may often make mistakes.

To us the basis for these professional norms is obvious, because Plato spelled it out with great care. The norms which define a role derive from the purposes it serves. The purpose of medicine, for example, is healing, and therefore being a real doctor means acting so as to achieve this aim. A man is a doctor when he cures his patients, but not when he makes them worse.[15]

These aims, it must be emphasised, are intrinsic to the roles, not just the aims and motives of individual people. Plato shows specifically that to define one's aim in terms of serving one's own interest creates confusion, but his painstaking argument makes out a more general case about the relations of roles to individual motives.[16] Doctors practise their profession in order to earn their living because, like other people, they have their own interest at heart, which means they acquire money to provide creature comforts, leisure, and security. Some groups of people may be greedier than others, and some may have distinctive interests; for example, young people may want to meet eligible partners, and civil servants may be preoccupied with security. Such information may well be worth collecting, but it has no direct bearing on our understanding of the roles in question. Being a shepherd means looking after sheep, not after oneself or one's family. I may *want* to be a doctor for the sake of money or reputation, but I can only *be* a doctor by adopting the aim written into the role, that is, by curing the sick.

It is important for the understanding of human and social life to look closely *at* the roles, their nature and relation to each other, for the tendency to look *behind* the role is very natural. The very metaphor suggests that there is an actor, as distinct from the role, and that it is him we want to know, unmasked by the social scientist. The officially defined roles of doctor, clergyman, or ruler are public images behind which we can discover personal motives, perhaps saintly devotion to the welfare of others or a desire for self-sacrifice behind the sober activities of the doctor; but we may look—and this is the more fashionable trend—into less reputable motives like greed or lust. Such lines of inquiry are perfectly proper as long as they do not make it appear that there is something sham about the roles themselves. Roles play a very real part in the working of society, and that is why we are specially indebted to Plato's analysis.

The real doctor or ruler is not a person, but what a person becomes or would become when, or if, he conforms perfectly to the demands of the role as defined by its intrinsic aims. Then he can be described as the ideal doctor or ruler, in the sense of distinguishing him from other people practising medicine or government as well as in the sense of embodying perfection. Roles represent norms which tell us how a man should act as a doctor, not how 'doctors' usually behave. Role definitions are normative.

But where do these norms or standards by which we judge if things are normal come from? Clearly they are not derived from what usually occurs, for the normal or 'proper' bank manager would not abscond with the customers' money even if many bank managers were to do so. Nor is the role an ideal in the sense of what people would like to be the case. Everybody may want bank managers to be fatherly and generous, but that does not make those traits part of the norm which defines the role of bank manager. The modern reader will not be at a loss to provide a basis for the kind of norms we have been talking about, and even if the answer seems obvious it must be stressed that such ideas had to be forged by great intellectual effort. The concept in question is that of function. At one level it is simple and obvious and was already familiar in Plato's time; but he explored it systematically, traced its metaphysical implications, pursued its epistemological consequences, and put its methodological fruitfulness to the test.

Bodily organs and tools are objects to which we can attribute functions without being speculative or controversial, and consequently they provide points of departure for Plato's arguments. One crucial passage (the interjections of agreement which give it the semblance of a dialogue are omitted here) begins thus:

> We can see only with our eyes and hear only with our ears so we can rightly call these the functions of eye and ear. Again, though we can cut a shoot from a vine with a carving-knife or chisel we would do the job best if we used a knife made for the purpose, which, surely, we may call its 'function'. And I think you may see now what I meant by asking if the 'function' of a thing was not that which only it can do or that which it can do best.[17]

The argument then goes on to suggest that each thing has its own excellence, which lies in its being able to fulfil its function well. It is in that sense that we use such phrases as 'good eyes' or 'a good knife'.[18] What has already been said about social roles readily falls into place. The aim or purpose which defines a role is its function. Plato invariably speaks about vocational roles, but there is no reason to think he would have resisted the extension of his theory to other social roles such as being a wife, a father, or a hostess.

Before we consider the use Plato makes of this functional approach it is worth noting how widely it is applied—far beyond what is obvious. We are warned about this in the introduction to the passage just quoted, where after stressing that the matter is not trivial, Plato asks, 'Do you think a horse has a function?'

When answered yes, he continues, 'And would you define it as something that only the horse (or whatever it may be) can do, or at any rate, that the horse does best?'[19] His interlocutor is puzzled, and Socrates then turns to bodily organs and tools. The horse is not mentioned again. But we have been given notice that the theory is meant to be applied to much more than parts of organic wholes, tools, or social roles which can be directly related to human purposes. We are even given a hint of how this may be done, but for the decisive exposition of the theory and its metaphysical grounding we must look at a later passage in the *Republic*, the important and difficult section on the Good.[20]

When the subject is first introduced, it appears to be simply the continuation and completion of the moral argument. In the preceding discussions of justice and the other cardinal virtues (wisdom, courage, and temperance), their traditional valuation had been accepted without question; but what tradition has hallowed and common sense approves still needs rational justification. To place morality on really firm philosophical foundations we must go back to a fundamental principle in terms of which particular virtues can be justified. It is not paradoxical or perverse to ask why when urged to be courageous or temperate. To be told that it is good to be courageous or that something good is achieved by temperance, is a final answer, though only a formal one. We still need an explanation of what makes something good or what the good is and this is *the* basic question of moral philosophy.

Had the discovery of an ultimate moral principle been all that was at issue, further development of the argument in the dialogue would make no sense whatever. But the moral argument is only one ingredient in a much more comprehensive theory. After dismissing any idea that the Good may be identified with either pleasure or knowledge, Socrates disclaims the ability to define it. That he could hardly do otherwise will become clear when we have completed our examination. Prevailed upon to give an indication of what he is talking about, he does so by means of an analogy, saying that the sun is the source of the light by which we see things and of the conditions in which plants and animals come to exist. It is also especially related to the eye, the organ of sight. In an analogous way the Good is the source of the existence of the intelligible world, makes it understandable, and is especially related to our faculty of knowing.

If the Good produces reality and makes it comprehensible, it must be more than a moral principle or ideal; it therefore makes sense to think of the Good in terms of function. This is what we mean when we ask what a thing is good for or what is the good of it, a point which can be most easily illustrated and made most convincing in terms of human products, physical or social. If we had to explain what a car was to someone who had never heard of one, we could not do so successfully by describing its parts, what they were made of, and how they were related to each other. The vital clue, without which no amount of explanation would make sense, is the function of a car, what it is good for, or what is the good of it. Each part can be explained in terms of its function, through which it contributes to the function of the car as a whole. All this is obvious but is sometimes overlooked in epistemological discussions. (A car works, so it is said, according to the laws of physics, and physics does not use functional explanations; this is correct but irrelevant.)

The same applies to such products of purposive human activity as social institutions. We could never understand what a university is by examining its buildings brick by brick, analysing the chemical consistency of blackboards or chairs, tabulating the number, weight, and size of human beings within the buildings, plotting their movements, and measuring the volume of sound coming from different rooms. There is no substitute for knowing the *function* of a university and considering the contribution which buildings and blackboards, laboratories and lecture halls, teachers and technicians, make to the fulfilment of this function.

It is not difficult to take the next step and show that the function of a thing, or what it is good for, is not only the principle for explaining it but the source and condition of its existence. Cars and universities have come into being because they were needed or wanted, that is, because they are good for something or fulfil a function.

So far we are on reasonably firm ground, but though Plato started from here, using tools and institutions—as well as physical organs and social roles—as intellectual models for his conception of function, he certainly did not stop there. We have already been warned by the reference to the horse. When he now says, 'The Good, therefore, may be said to be the source not only of the intelligibility of the objects of knowledge, but also of their existence and reality,'[21] he is certainly not talking about human products but extrapolating a principle which has proved its value in a limited sphere of experience into a universal one. But this does not mean that his approach is an idle game with ideas. The theory answers some intellectual needs by providing a framework for answering pertinent questions.

A petrol pump can best be explained in terms of the contribution it makes to fulfilling the function of a motorcar. It is intelligible as part of a system of interrelated subfunctions. Since the same is true of the laboratory in the university, it is not far-fetched to try to understand the function of a car or university as a subfunction in a yet larger system, say the economic or social life of man. When we extrapolate this line of thought, we must conclude that the maximum intellectual satisfaction would only be possible if the whole of reality formed a single functional system. Modern thought has largely discounted this point of view. To ask what the function of a horse or the ocean is, seems odd if not ridiculous to us, but we may think it less so if we remember that even today any religious person believes, as Plato did nearly 2,400 years ago, that the universe is purposively constructed by a good and just God and forms an ordered whole or cosmos. What may remain controversial, even among the pious, is whether the divine plan can or cannot be gauged by human beings.

It is Plato's central thesis that the Good is the supreme or final aim towards which the universe works and in terms of which everything is ordered, so that each thing has its place and role defined by the contribution it makes to the whole. However, even Plato was not so bold as to state categorically what the purpose of the universe is, and Socrates shrank from the issue, resorting to the analogy of the sun.

The concept of the Good cannot therefore be used as an explanatory principle in the sense in which the idea of healing can be used to explain the specific activities of the doctor, or that of self-propelled motion the function of cylinders, pistons, wheels,

and crankshafts in a car. But this does not rob it of all significance. There remains the guiding and heuristic idea of function
itself. We may not know the final aim to which everything contributes, and possibly could only know it as a final result of
endless research, but we are encouraged to look for the function
of things if we are convinced that they are designed for some
purpose.

How the investigator proceeds is already indicated in the quotation about the horse. We can look at an object and recognise,
in an ordinary, empirical way, the significant features which
distinguish it from other objects, and then ask, What is it that
can only be done, or done better, because of these characteristics?—which is a matter of empirical investigation. If you come
across an unusual knife and do not know what it is for, you
may note the features which distinguish it from other knives,
discover that they make it especially suitable for pruning vines,
and conclude that it is a pruning knife.[22] Here the method is
noncontroversial, because we know that tools like knives have
a function. In fact, as Plato also suggests in his later discussion
of the bed,[23] we can refer to the men who have made these tools
with a purpose in mind or consult the user who has asked for
it to be made to meet his requirements. However, Plato is equally
prepared to use his method when there is no independent evidence of a purpose. When he applies it to man we find it, not
surprisingly, of particular interest, for it concerns us all as human
beings who wonder what life is all about. In that sense Plato's
method is important to the philosopher as a basis for morality
and directly relevant for the student of society.

This line of thought opens the way for a functional exploration
of human nature and, at the same time, suggests the need for
a normative definition of being a man, which in this sense, like
being a doctor, means playing a role. Everyday speech does not
conform to this conception consistently, because we usually
identify creatures as human beings on purely factual, that is,
biological, criteria just as we call people doctors and teachers
according to their qualifications and the type of work they do.
But we would not do justice to some of our thinking if we did
not introduce normative role definitions. Just as we say that a
bungling practitioner who harms his patients is not really a doc-

tor, so we can say that a person is not a man but a monster. As a purely descriptive definition this would be absurd, because every creature with the physical characteristics of a man would be a man, and whatever he did would be a human action. But because we think of being a man as a role to be played properly or not, we must strive to be fully human and if we fail may become subhuman. Virtue means acting as a man is meant to act; self-realisation is not just being oneself, but becoming what one can and should be. Thus, when Plato defines man as a rational being,[24] he does not express the shallow, optimistic, belief that people are usually rational (his work is full of vivid descriptions of unbridled passion, savagery, and beastliness) but maintains that the norm for man is to be governed by his reason.

Plato's normative approach can be pursued into the more recondite reaches of his metaphysics and theory of knowledge. It may well be that his theory of forms has its roots, at least partly, in his desire to understand the social world in terms of types of roles normatively defined. This theory of forms, the keystone of Plato's philosophy, is complex and controversial. Plato believed that genuine knowledge must refer to pure and unchanging objects and that if the object was not pure, its definition would be lost in endless qualifications.[25] Similarly, if the object were to be involved in a process of change, our information would be false the next moment. True knowledge is therefore not directly about the messy, complex, and changing world of our senses but about pure thought objects—the forms—which lie behind this world as a model for approximation.

As geometry may well have been the inspiration of the theory of forms, it can provide us with an illustration. The circular objects we encounter in daily life and the circles we draw on blackboards are not the circles which are the subject matter of geometry. The latter conform strictly to a definition which lays down what a circle should be and are not only the ideal and perfect, but also the real, circles, of which blackboard circles or circular tables are only an imitation or approximation. Our knowledge of circles (such as that every point is equidistant from the centre) applies only to the object of the geometer's thought. The rim of the circular table is inevitably uneven and subject to change, such as buckling in the heat.

The world of mathematics appeared to Plato, as it has to many other philosophers, as a luminously ordered sphere, the knowledge of which, by its precision, clarity and certainty, provided a paradigm for all cognitive processes. Thus he treats the relation between the real doctor and the men who practise medicine, between the real man and the people we encounter in daily life, as analogous to that between the real circle and circular objects. In each case the former is the true object of knowledge and provides the norm to which the latter merely approximate. Hence the study of man and society, so important for Plato, can aspire to the same certainty as mathematics.

Ultimately this conception can be extended until it covers all class-names (though Plato has misgivings about going the whole way). The definition of a horse or a daffodil, a diamond or a river, prescribes the essential qualities a thing should possess to deserve its name, though the creatures we call by that name only approximate to the ideal type. Thus we may say that the forms are ideal roles which empirical objects play more or less adequately. Of course, it is not pussy's aim to be a cat, because for Plato the purpose of an object is defined by the role assigned to it within the purposive order of the universe, and not by what it wants. In the case of man, an individual's personal aim, that is, the personal motive from which he acts, may, or may not, coincide with the purpose inherent in the professional role he has chosen. He may want to be a good doctor, that is, what a doctor is meant to be; on the other hand his chief aim may be to make money or achieve success, and he will fulfil the doctor's function of curing the sick for his own purpose. This distinction between the purpose inherent in a role (or its function) and the actor's motive is important for the sociologist, as it wil govern the kind of explanations he seeks.

According to Plato's hypothesis that the intelligible universe represents a functional whole, the forms must be functionally related in a system, the organising principles of which are the highest forms, namely those of goodness, truth, and beauty.[26] The underlying reality is therefore functionally perfect, intellectually transparent, and aesthetically harmonious. The special importance of justice lies in the fact that it is the principle which governs the relation between norms and the roles which they

define. It is thus a meta-norm, or norm of norms, and hence
the subject of one of Plato's most important dialogues. 'Justice',
he explains there, 'is minding one's own business' and 'keeping
to what belongs to one and doing one's own job'; he adds that
'the provision that the man naturally fitted to be a shoemaker,
or carpenter, or anything else, should stick to his own trade has
turned out to be a kind of image of justice'.[27]

Ideal Types in the Description of Societies and Personalities

Plato applied his ideas of role, function, and their place in a
teleological system as methodological tools for the analysis of
human nature and social life. To these he adds another powerful
methodological concept derived from his theory of forms: the
construction of ideal types. It is no accident that the theory of
forms has a direct bearing on the understanding of the social
world. Though the theory is a metaphysical account of ultimate
reality and a contribution to logic, it was also designed from the
outset to provide signposts for the study of changeable social
and political circumstances.

The theory of forms explains how we can achieve reliable
knowledge, by postulating that true reality consists of very general patterns to which empirical facts merely approximate. The
Republic brings out the methodological implications of this view,
for its most striking feature—which gave the dialoque its name—
is the construction of an ideal society. Here the meaning is partly
moral, for Plato constructs a model which he puts forward for
imitation if we are to improve society and its citizens. But it is
also ideal in the sense that it is a thought construction which is
not derived from observation or likely to be fully achieved by
human effort in the future. At one point in the dialogue, Glaucon, speaking of 'the society which we have been describing
and which we have theoretically founded', says, 'I doubt if it
will ever exist on earth'. Socrates replies, 'Perhaps it is laid up
as a pattern in heaven, where those who wish can see it and
found it in their own hearts. But it does not matter whether it
exists or ever will exist.'[28]

That this construction is both a moral idea and a theoretical
model for the comprehension of existing societies can best be

seen in the section of the *Republic* in which Plato compares his ideal society with models of different forms of society.[29] The pictures of timarchy (a type of military rule), oligarchy (the rule of the rich), democracy (the rule of the people), and tyranny (the rule of one man for his own ends) are certainly not moral ideals offered for imitation, but neither are they empirical descriptions of particular societies. There is nothing of the incidental and idiosyncratic features, the products of geography or history, in these pen-portraits. Absent too is the conflict of complex personalities, the confusion of clashing norms, and the uncertainty of imperfectly played roles which characterise actual societies. Yet Plato's examples are related to, and intended to explain, existing social arrangements.

Plato describes the relationship between the different forms of society in terms of a continuous decline from the ideal society to tyranny, each society containing the seed of its own destruction. The ideal society, governed by wisdom, embodied in the rule of philosophers, declines into timarchy, which is based on the principles of honour, discipline, and patriotism. Plato is vague on how this first decline occurs; the ideal society, functioning (by definition) perfectly, should not be unstable. There is the added difficulty that nothing approximating such a society has ever existed, so that there is no empirical evidence how it could decline. Still, Plato assumes, rather unconvincingly, that wisdom is lost.

Having reached timarchy he is on firmer ground, for when honour, a subsidiary principle in the ideal society, becomes dominant, it is seen to be self-destructive, because it leads to arrogance, ambition, and various frustrations. Timarchy then declines into oligarchy, in which wealth, held in check in the preceding societies, becomes the dominant principle. As wealth is concentrated in fewer and fewer hands and the growing army of the poor becomes poorer, the rule of the rich proves self-defeating, and society breaks up into two nations without a common interest. Some of the poor become functionless—a *Lumpenproletariat*—and must either be maintained by the state or turn to crime. A divided society is ill-equipped for war and ripe for revolution. (Here readers will recognise a brilliant anticipation of Marxist arguments and note the origin of Disraeli's famous reference to 'two nations'.) Democracy, based on the principle of liberty, results when the poor strip the small number of rich of power, reject all authority—of rulers, judges, policemen, parents or teachers—and abandon all discipline and obedience to rules. This lack of law (or anomy as Durkheim has called it)[30] produces an unstable society, open to subversion and the establishment of autocratic tyranny, where liberty is transformed into its opposite: enslavement to the wanton will of an individual.

The details in this series of vignettes—the thickheadedness of military rulers, the divisiveness of wealth as a governing principle, the trend toward permissiveness within democracies, and the way in which dictators usurp and maintain power—are brilliantly perceptive and staggeringly prophetic. Today we, who have witnessed the rise of several dictators and radical democracies, can appreciate, far better than our grandparents, the strength of the theories which Plato developed from his (relatively) narrow experience more than two millenia ago. We can only appreciate the full significance of what Plato attempted when we realise that the story of political systems declining and changing into each other is a theoretical construct and not history, moral fable, or philosophy of history; no actual societies are mentioned. Even if we argued that specific societies are still recognisable behind the thin disguise of his generalised descriptions, we would still be confronted by the insuperable objection that the whole sequence begins with an ideal society which has never existed.

Plato is undoubtedly illustrating moral issues in his picture of decline: the first society is morally the best, the last the worst. (On the intermediary societies he is less clear, and there is no definite indication that he considered democracy morally inferior to oligarchy.) This does not mean that he believed moral decline was inevitable. His sustained moral fervour proves this, for it would be absurd for him to call for a reversal to a development thought irreversible.

There is also no evidence that Plato's description of political change represents a theory about stages of history like those of Vico and Comte, or historical laws of the type Hegel and Marx suggested. For him ideals were timeless models to be imitated and striven for throughout the fluctuating course of human affairs, and not something which history moves towards or away from.

As Plato's presentation is neither history nor philosophy of history, neither pessimistic comment nor moral fable, we can accept it more readily as an exercise in sociological analysis. An analogy with the more formally elaborated physical sciences is useful, though one must remember that Plato's approach preceded the development of similar methods in physics by many centuries. The law of physics do not refer directly to observable events but to ideal states such as free fall or frictionless movement, which we can never encounter. Thus if we want to account for actual events such as the downward drift of falling leaves or the movement of wheels on the road, we must dilute the purity of these laws by introducing subsidiary laws and specific facts.

This is precisely what Plato was doing when he envisaged the ideal society, the pure, frictionless state free from outside interference, a complete system working according to its own norms with perfect functional efficiency. To transform this ideal model into one capable of explaining how specific societies actually work, it is necessary to introduce, one by one, specific factors and subsidiary principles which reflect forces operating in society. The original rational structure of the ideal society is thereby demolished and replaced progressively by others which are less and less functionally adequate. Timarchy, oligarchy, democracy, and tyranny are unstable, because they are based on defective principles which, when consistently adhered to, produce friction, conflict, and the ultimate replacement of one social arrangement by another. In this way Plato spelled out dynamic laws governing the conduct of human affairs (such as 'The pursuit of wealth divides societies' and 'Democracies are unstable and lead to dictatorships') and so laid bare the mechanisms of social and political change.

If theories are to have an explanatory value, the principles used must, like Plato's, be realistic. For love of honour, greed for money, or love of liberty are motives of human action. But the theory as a whole is not a description of what can be observed, because we do not encounter individuals or societies exclusively moved by only one motive. By producing these simplified models of how a society would function if based on a single principle, unaffected by external influences, Plato is constructing what Weber came to call 'ideal types'.[31]

Parallel with, and supplementing, this theory of ideal types of societies, Plato employed the same concepts, organising principles, and dynamic laws to produce a typology of personalities. He did this deliberately to underscore and utilise the interdependence between personalities and societies, which do not acquire a particular character through any mysterious process but because people of a certain type run them or are dominant in them. If there were no greedy people, there could not be a greedy society. In turn, a society encourages the development of personalities which fit into it; a commercially oriented society promotes and rewards commercially minded men, a militaristic society, soldierly men.

Plato's personality types are defined in terms of the predominant motive which determines their actions and are constructed as ideal types in the same way as his societies. The philosopher acts from knowledge and reason; rational reflection controls and harmonises all his impulses. The timarchic man, Plato's man of military virtues, is prompted by such motives as honour, ambition, and service to his country. His self-discipline springs from these sentiments, but they do not—because they are not based on reason—prevent him from being arrogant to his inferiors or indulging in secret vices when out of the public eye. The oligarchic man is orientated towards economic activity and profit-making, the entrepreneurial type. His virtues of industry, frugality, and honesty are a matter of utility and respectability rather than moral aspirations. The democratic man is anomic; he gives way to every impulse as it arises and is easy-going, entertaining, and unreliable. Finally, the tyrannical man is one in whom an unbridled passion—greed, sexual desire, or aggression—has gained dominance over his whole mental life. Each type of man displays some of the potentialities inherent in human nature, including the reason of the philosopher or the monstrous passions of the tyrant; yet they are, essentially, cultural types shaped by a social process. The oligarchic man, for example, is not just a person who happens to like money, but one who believes that the pursuit of money is a worthwhile goal because he has received this cultural norm from a particular tradition and environment.

Personalities dominated by a single cultural norm are ideal types, because actual human beings are more complex and inconsistent, and people are mixed types or change type in the course of time or in different situations. A man who channels all his energies into the pursuit of wealth may turn into a democratic, which in this case means permissive and self-indulgent, man in old age; or when he returns from his office he may be a tyrant at home. One must also remember that the types are not puppets with single motives but exhibit a combination of motives in which one is dominant. The ideal philosopher is not a man without passion or ambition (a very dull automaton), but controls passion and ambition with reason.

All that has been said about the typology of societies could be repeated about personality types. The philosopher is the perfectly functional man, fulfilling the function of being a man or playing the role assigned to him in the cosmic scheme; he does this because every aspect of his personality performs its proper function. Each of the other types is defined in terms of less adequate organising principles, which lead to malfunctioning.

That Plato's pictures of societies and personalities are ideal types and not realistic portraits gives them their heuristic value; but we must remember when we employ them that they do not identify actual societies. We shall never meet a 'real' oligarch, only men who have some oligarchic features such as uncontrolled cravings and a desire for honour. Similarly there are no democracies, in Plato's sense, for though a country like Britain is democratic insofar as it is committed to the freedom of individuals, it also has oligarchic and timocratic features and even those of an ideal society to the extent to which reason rules in the shape of experts and scientific advisers. Plato's typology is relevant, but it must be used with care and discretion, because such hypotheses as that democracy leads to dictatorship cannot be applied to Britain as if they were predictions. Yet by drawing attention to the mechanisms at work in society, the typology points to possibilities which needs watching.

Human Nature

To determine how man should live, Plato needed an idea of what man was like, and this meant that he had to determine both how man functions and his function in the universe. In terms of this analysis Plato also explained what justice is and why it is important. For him justice is playing one's part properly and thereby fulfilling one's function in society and, for that matter, in the universe.

Plato saw man as a composite creature, consisting of mind and body, of an immortal soul linked to an animal body. Being austere, puritanical, and high-minded, he took a rather dim view of this entanglement of spirit in matter, and his enormous influence has left its mark on the intellectual life of Europe. In Christian theology it inspired the conception that the body is the prison of the soul and encouraged asceticism. As part of the theory of knowledge it led many to assign a low value to sense experience and physical experiments. Today, when people do not need to be warned against neglecting their bodies because of preoccupation with their souls, there is no practical urgency about counteracting this Platonic influence. Nor must we plead with scientists to do more observing and less speculating; if anything, Plato's theories may now serve as a useful corrective. But all this does not affect the rest of his own analysis.

In his study of man Plato first focusses on the way man can be prompted to action. He distinguishes three types of motives, or groups of motives, starting with the instincts and urges which spring from our animal nature and physical needs.[32] There is nothing startling about his account except the perceptiveness with which he anticipates quite modern insights, suggesting, for example, that dreams reflect the unbridled savagery of our urges.[33] The second group of motives contains such sentiments as pride, shame, and ambition, which though they are not rational, cannot be aligned with the instincts. They do not appear to have a physiological basis or to fulfill an obvious function in the life of man the animal (pride, for example, can be both foolish and contrary to our instincts). But they are clearly of special interest to the observer of social life. The third source of motives for action is reason, which Plato believes could determine conduct.

   Applying to this conception of man the type of analysis we
have already discussed, Plato arrives at the following conclusions (as Aristotle did more explicitly after him). Man shares
being alive and having certain bodily functions with plants and
animals; he shares instincts and some motives, like pride, with
animals; but reason is man's unique and distinguishing endowment. It follows that what can only be done (or best done) by
reason—that is, reflection, the acquisition of knowledge, and
the rational ordering of conduct—represents man's function in
the scheme of things. By using reason he fulfills his function
and himself; he becomes most fully human or a good man.[34]
The question how man can fulfill his function as man obviously
refers to the moral sphere, a special case of proper functioning.
A good man is good by virtue of being what a man is meant to
be, just as a knife is good when it functions well.
   This conclusion hinges partly on the function of reason itself,
and Plato uses his characteristic argument to answer the question
why it should be reason rather than instinct or love of honour
which is designed to control conduct. Reason is the faculty of
judgement;[35] it is part of its nature to weigh, balance, anticipate,
and adjudicate. The instincts, in contrast, are blind; they may
prompt man to excesses detrimental to his health and happiness
or conflict with each other and produce frustration. Thus it is
the role of reason to dominate, control and harmonise all the
factors determining human conduct.[36]
   Plato applied his functional approach to the relation between
personality and society and highlighted the way human conduct
was socially determined. In the early part of the *Republic* both
Thrasymachus and Glaucon imply that society is merely a constraint upon the individual. The former sees it as a pattern of
relations imposed on the population by a ruling class in its own
interest; for Glaucon society is the arrangement by which individuals are protected from the horrors of jungle law by making
a compromise.[37] Underlying both views is the conception that
other people are a nuisance or even a menace and that unfor-
tunately, since we must live among our fellows, power relations
must be settled by struggle or compromise to end the war of all
against all. Instead of criticising the arguments underlying this
view, Socrates offers an alternative conception, that society is a

necessary condition and means of human self-realisation. We are essentially social beings who can only fulfill ourselves in society.

The basic necessities of human life, but even more the conditions for cultured and civilised living, can only be assured through cooperation and exchange of services, large and complex enterprises, such as the building of cities, requiring joint effort. Again, we depend on each other because of the different capacities (mathematical gifts, physical strength, or good eyesight) which help us to excel in one type of work or another. It is best for all of us if we can develop these gifts and concentrate on what we can do well. By providing a stable basis for the division of labour and cooperation which it makes necessary, society fulfills the function it alone can perform, of making a fully human life possible.[38]

This theory suggests a very close relationship between personality and society, the former being shaped by social forces, the latter reflecting human purposes and capacities. Throughout the *Republic* Plato talks of the two in parallel terms, stating quite early that 'justice can be a characteristic of an individual or of a community'.[39] To illuminate the subject of justice in the individual, he starts with a discussion of a just society, suggesting that to treat the individual first is analogous to a shortsighted man's being 'set to read a distant notice written in small letters' and discovering that 'the same notice is up elsewhere on a larger scale and in larger lettering'. 'Won't it be a godsend to us', he continues, 'to be able to read the larger notice first and then compare it with the smaller, to see if they are the same?'[40]

Neither in the passage quoted nor anywhere else does Plato suggest that society is some kind of superperson with thoughts or interests, virtues or vices, other than those which arise from the qualities and actions of its citizens. Of course, he talks of wise or foolish, acquisitive, brave, or happy societies, but he knows that these qualities derive from the wisdom, courage, or acquisitiveness of human individuals—though for him this was not a matter of statistics. To say that the more brave citizens there are, the braver the society, is not only too simple but positively misleading. One must look at the structure of society in terms of functions and ask what role certain types of individuals play; a society cannot be called wise merely because a lot of its citizens are so, only when wise men are involved in the decisions which are fundamental to its nature and direction. Similarly a society is brave if brave men defend it, not if a lot of people face the dentist without shrinking.[41] It follows that a society can change its character without any of its citizens' changing theirs; it only requires changes in social structure, new people coming to the top or playing new roles. When those best fitted to do so—the wise—rule, and that rule is readily accepted, a society is just; a man is just when the faculty best fitted to control his actions—his reason—prevails.

The characteristics of its citizens shape society in various ways and are reflected in it; society makes provision for food production or artistic activity because its people need food and want beautiful objects, and is determined by the type of people who play important roles in it.

On the other hand Plato believed that personality is shaped and that human beings with their different natural characteristics are moulded and controlled by society, a point made in his ponderous joke about the philosphical dog.[42] The dog loves knowledge for he is friendly to those he knows but savage to strangers; if even a dog can be trained and his aggression directed towards special objects, then human beings must surely be educable. Indeed, education is one of Plato's main themes, though the purely intellectual side of it is of least interest to the student of sociology. Plato believed in free argument[43] and that education brought something out of the student rather than putting it in, liberating him from prejudices and turning him in the right direction rather than giving him information.[44] The nonrational aspects of man, sexual desire and fear, aggression and pride, are present in all of us, child and adult, when reason is little developed. It is here, Plato argues, that education and the physical environment—beautiful or ugly sights, comfort or hardship—music, exercise and, above all, stories, plays, and poems have their influence. Even the games children play, the gymnastic exercises they are made to perform, and the kind of songs they are exposed to are all character-forming: hence Plato's notorious proposals for an austere censorship of literature, particularly for children.[45] The discussions he initiated have continued to this day; we still worry about the influence of pornography, horror comics, or television violence—the modern version of Plato's basic problem, the influence of corrupt art on unformed minds. He is full of fascinating theories about this, most of which have remained unconfirmed and unrefuted to this day, particularly intriguing being his hypothesis that acting, the regular assumption of various roles, undermines the integrity of character.

As well as education in the wider sense, in school or in the cultural atmosphere outside the classroom, the importance of the family is stressed in the shaping of personality. When he discusses the different personality types, Plato paints some delightful pictures of how relations within a family and the outlook of the father determine the personality of his children in a way which is predictable but more subtle than could be accounted for by imitation or reaction.[46] In one of these vignettes of family life,[47] the father is what Plato calls a democratic man, which we might call a liberal or, more recently, a 'permissive' man. He believes in doing what one pleases and brings up his son without any discipline. Having no principles to help him resist temptation, the son may easily be dominated by desire or passion, set on this path by the example and influence of criminal types bound to flourish in a society which encourages greed and does not believe in restraints even for delinquents.

Turning to the more general pressures by which society forms personality, Plato speaks of the corrupting influence of a corrupt society on potential philosophers.[48] But the point is really a general one, for he asks why the most able and strong-minded members of society are so frequently preoccupied with matters other than those for which they are admirably fitted, namely, the pursuit of knowledge and its use for the benefit of society, and concludes that their motives are determined by social rewards and punishments. Any society, whatever its dominant preoccupations, will want to gain the zealous cooperation of the able and active; if it values commerce it will tempt and cajole potential leaders with money and honours and deter those who might go into scholarship with threats of poverty and contempt. Such pressures may be exercised by special institutions or members of the ruling class, but they may also emanate from public opinion, which, as Plato saw, becomes dominant when society has no thought-out priorities or if its education is concerned with opinion rather than knowledge.

Plato also comments shrewdly on the way roles affect motives and thus character. His proposal that in an ideal society the guardians should not be permitted to have stable marriages is well known.[49] Then, as it does now, it seemed a shocking proposal, flying in the face of human nature and its needs. But Plato is not concerned with feasibility, rather with the point that family loyalties run counter to, and are destructive of, wider loyalties to society. Perhaps looking after your wife becomes more important than serving your country; or you want a good job for your son, even if he is not the best man for it; you come to believe that achieving these aims is an overriding duty. To the individual a collective, family, selfishness appears as unselfishness. It is interesting that Plato is not content to educate people about priorities in loyalty, but proposes to abolish or alter family roles in order to prevent their deleterious influence. As he is so much, and rightly, associated with an educational approach, it should be emphasised that here, as in his proposal for abolishing private property among the guardian class,[50] Plato unhesitatingly turns to structural changes in society in order to create the personality types he wants and thus to assure the desired attitudes.

When people fall short in their roles, it is frequently not because some instinct escapes control or some personal idiosyncracy refuses to be subdued, but because another role is exercising its pull and interfering with the proper performance of the first one. The role of husband and father, for instance, may turn out to be inconsistent with that of military leader. Hence Plato's belief in the radical re-structuring of society.

Plato's immense influence on sociology is not easily measured. It is arguable that sociology, like philosophy (as Whitehead said), is a series of footnotes to his work. Certainly his reflections display an incredible power of observation and a genius for generating a host of interesting social hypotheses, of which 'childrens' games shape their 'personality' and 'societies exert pressures on gifted individuals in order to impose on them socially accepted ideals', are but two. Equally important are his insistence that science involves the use of theoretical concepts and his success in developing and systematically relating to each other a number of such useful concepts as role, function, and ideal type. That these hypotheses and methodological devices are tightly linked together and supported by a comprehensive metaphysical scheme may appear to the sociology student an irritant rather than an asset. Sceptical of philosophical flights he may consider the pragmatic, ad hoc development of concepts and theories preferable. He should ask himself, though, if this is not the attitude which has left sociology open to the charge that it is a woolly subject, a soft option. Could it be that sociology gives this impression because it does not sufficiently define and justify its presuppositions? Even if we cannot accept Plato's conclusions, they give us an idea of the kind of broad framework we need if our castles of theory are not to sink ingloriously into their muddy foundations.

3 • *Descartes*: The Quest for Certainty

In the seventeenth century Descartes took up the torch of reason by insisting relentlessly on the need to justify all claims to knowledge and asking how we gain objectivity and certainty. His influence encouraged subsequent generations to be rigorous in their science and restrained in their speculations. His own concern with reason and scientific stringency arose from and reflected the social and intellectual ferment which in his time (1596-1650) pervaded Western Europe. By then the unity of Western Christianity that characterised the Middle Ages had largely disintegrated, the Protestantism of Calvin, Zwingli, and Luther had gained many adherents, and Europe was split into warring religious factions, a conflict that culminated in the devastating Thirty Years' War. For thoughtful men the collapse of the universal authority of the church and mortal conflict between Christians was a traumatic experience.

Yet at the same time other factors were at work in changing men's outlook and ushering in a new world to which we are the direct heirs. The new Humanism, inspired by renewed study of ancient Greek literature, and the Renaissance spreading from Italy, combined to emphasise the value and beauty of earthly life and the right of man to enjoy it; men turned from religious fanaticism, preoccupation with life after death, and spiritual salvation to the problems of this world. This new interest also laid the foundations of modern science. In astronomy and physics, chemistry, and biology, solidly based progress was made which radically changed man's view of his environment.

Descartes was very much affected by and involved in these developments. He was a Catholic and educated by the Jesuits, but to find peace for his work he lived for twenty years in the more tolerant climate of Protestant Holland. Though he always professed himself a faithful son of the church and, in his philosophy was concerned to prove the existence of God and an immaterial soul, he was tolerant, urbane, and reasonable, sceptical of fanaticism, and worldly in his interests. He travelled widely to acquire experience and took part in one of the campaigns of the Thirty Years' War. Above all he had a consuming interest in the new scientific developments and actively participated in them, his greatest contribution being the development of Cartesian geometry, in which he showed himself a mathematician of genius. He also worked on some problems of physics, such as the atomic structure of matter and the character of natural motion, as well as those of biology, like the circulation of the blood and the function of various organs. Because of his personal involvement in both camps, he was deeply disturbed by the clash between church and science. He had been a child when Giordano Bruno was burned by the Inquisition for his belief in the multiplicity of worlds,[1] and in his late thirties when he heard the (for him) shattering news that it had forced Galileo to renounce his adherence to the Copernican theory.[2] Descartes's philosophy is an intensely personal attempt to achieve clarity and certainty in the face of the conflicting points of view around him as well as in his own mind. Some of its originality and appeal lies in its being presented as the intellectual autobiography of a man trying to emerge from doubt. His rationalism is not based on facile blindness to the power of irrational forces but, on the contrary, springs from an urgent desire to overcome the divisive forces of superstition, prejudice, bigotry, and fanaticism by the use of reason. The conflict between religion and science could not be resolved by assigning to each a sphere where it could reign supreme. In exploring physical reality, science could not subvert faith however far it pushed its inquiries, because it could not affect belief in God and an immortal soul revealed by religion and supported by reason.

A purely rational approach involved, as he believed, a radical break with tradition, with beliefs that had been accepted for no better reason than that they had been held for a long time or produced by distinguished authors in the past. By insisting that it was more important to observe and experiment, to examine and think for oneself than to reread the thinkers of the past reverently, he voiced the new scientific spirit. Called, with some justice, the father of modern philosophy, Descartes was also the pioneer of views which were to become dominant in the Western world, i.e., the right of individuals to question and inquire freely and follow their own chosen way. He foresaw and welcomed the unimpeded forward march of science and even envisaged its application to the control of nature; he was, in fact, a prophet of the coming age of technology.

But at the very centre was his interest in epistemology. For him the questions What can we know? and How do we know it? took pride of place over all others inside or outside philosophy. Pursuit of the theory of knowledge was not new in itself, but Descartes's insistence that philosophy must start with these questions was revolutionary and set the tone for most modern philosophy. That we must ask of any statement, How do you know that it is true and why are you so sure? is essential if any study of nature or of man is to be scientific. That is why the purely philosophical arguments which embody his theory of knowledge are of considerable interest even to nonphilosophers.

Descartes's main epistemological position can be outlined fairly easily and briefly because he has sketched it sharply and elegantly in his *Discourse on Method* (mainly part 4) and his *Meditations*. When he looked at what passed for knowledge around him—the traditional disciplines such as philosophy and history taught in the schools and the opinions and views he shared with his contemporaries—he was dismayed to find that they lacked the hallmark of truth. The differences between philosophic schools, the divergence of views among sensible people of different civilisations and ages, suggested that they rested on uncertain foundations, that the basis of what we unthinkingly call knowledge had not been properly examined and consolidated.[3]

Descartes addressed himself to this problem using mathematics as his model of what certain knowledge should be like.[4]

First he had to find a certain, self-evident starting point and then to reason cogently and carefully, step by step, to true conclusions which might tally with our previous beliefs but were transformed by this process into solid knowledge. To this model of what the establishment of certainty should be like he added a methodological canon which constitutes what has been called the analytical method.

His first rule is to take nothing for granted but to accept only what is clearly, distinctly, and therefore self-evidently true or based on indubitable evidence. The second rule is to divide any problem 'into as many parts as are required to solve it'. The third is to think in an orderly way by building up arguments from the simple to the complex. The fourth is to check the completeness of the argument.[5] Descartes concludes:

> Those long chains of reasons, all quite simple and quite easy, which geometers are wont to employ in reaching their most difficult demonstrations, had given me occasion to imagine that all the possible objects of human knowledge were linked together in the same way, and that, if we accepted none as true that was not so in fact, and kept the right order in deducing one from the other, there was nothing so remote that it could not be reached, nothing so hidden that it could not be discovered.[6]

Today we have become reluctant to accept this classical expression of the philosophy of reason at its most confident. Even the other part of the theory, the brick-and-mortar conception of knowledge, is controversial, though it has played an enormous part in the history of science, not least the social sciences. Just as you build wholes from their parts or build houses from bricks, you can begin to understand complex things by coming to know their simpler components and their relation to each other. There is obviously something to be said for this theory, but it can also be argued that frequently we first understand the complex whole and then the parts in the lights of that whole. Certainly this latter view has contributed to the development of the social sciences, and its sharp rejection in Descartes's theory is itself of historical significance.

When he applied his analytical method to his philosophic

enquiry and had to look for a starting point, Descartes availed himself of the method of systematic doubt. This meant that he added to his real uncertainties, based on different opinions among authorities and lack of well-argued foundations, other, purely theoretical arguments derived from the history of philosophy. They showed up the lack of stringent, logical foundations for our common beliefs, which he also doubted. Our senses often deceive us, he said, so how can we be sure on any particular occasion that we are correctly informed? Sometimes we dream so vividly that we think we are awake, confronted with the situation we are only dreaming about. Can I even be sure that I am awake and not dreaming that I am writing? Again, since we may make mistakes in our reasoning (for example, doing sums), can we ever rely on our reason?[7] Finally, Descartes introduced the idea of the arch-deceiver, a demon who constantly deceives us.[8] In other words, he suggested that the universe may be constructed in such a way that our faculties are inadequate and we are constantly deceived (a nightmare to which we have been made more receptive by modern propaganda machines).

Descartes presents a formidable array of sceptical guns, and it might be said that if we really took his arguments seriously we would despair of knowledge. If we do not know when we are reasoning wrongly, no reasoning can be relied on, and if there is an arch-deceiver, any argument which disproves his existence may be part of the deception. It can also be argued that these sceptical arguments are not fully meaningful. What can error or deception mean when we cannot compare it with correct observation? What would it mean to dream if we cannot tell when we are awake? Descartes uses these sceptical arguments dramatically to create a philosophic mood, but he insists that they are purely theoretical aids and soft-pedals one or the other when it is necessary to get his own positive arguments going.[9]

What emerged triumphantly—and fatefully for the history of modern thought—from this mood of doubt was the certainty of consciousness about its own existence. Doubting, making mistakes, being deceived, are all states of consciousness and testify to the existence of the consciousness which doubts or is deceived. The fact that that which thinks, or is conscious, is also aware of being conscious is grammatically expressed by 'I'. The statement 'It thinks, therefore it is' is logically correct, but the premise can be doubted. In 'I think' the premise is indubitably given.[10]

Precisely what we have when we have established this I or consciousness which exists in mental activities and mental content must be made clear. At this moment, hungry and a little cold, I am aware of sitting on a chair by my desk, looking out of the window at grey streets and thinking about Descartes's theories. Other ideas are at the edge of my consciousness: sounds in the house and convictions about a great variety of things, for example, who I am and how old I am. This bundle of awareness constitutes my consciousness, the 'I' we have been talking about. If I were asked, Do you really think that you are at your desk? Do you feel cold? I would answer yes without any doubt, for not only am I certain of my existence as a consciousness, but certain of its content. But let us be quite clear what it is that is in doubt. I am certain that I have visual images of a street, but can I say that there is a street outside? No; it is logically possible that I am deceived by an illusion or that I am dreaming, or perhaps hypnotized into thinking that I see what is not there. Both the past which I remember and the identity which I ascribe to myself may also be an illusion. It might be extremely unlikely, but it is not logically impossible to think that I have been brainwashed into thinking that I am another person.

The gulf between what is within consciousness and what may be outside is fixed, and when we use such words as 'see', 'hear', or 'remember', the sentences we form have a double meaning. When I say 'I see an elephant', I am describing a state of my consciousness, giving an autobiographical account of the image or images in front of me, and I am certain that no one can talk me out of it. But in common usage, I also mean 'There is an elephant over there', and in this I can be mistaken, for it may be a hallucination or a clever representation or any of the other possibilities conjured up by Descartes's systematic doubt. In everyday life we do not usually distinguish between these two meanings except in very special cases, as when the oculist is interested in what you *see* and not in what is there. Normally we see an elephant because there is an elephant. The former is the evidence for the latter, the latter the cause of the former.

In sociology the distinction between how people perceive a situation and what the situation is, is highly significant because interpretations which are false or flimsily supported play a much larger part in our lives than optical illusions. 'A lot of people see foreign immigration as a menace' is certainly not identical with 'Foreign immigration is a menace' and either may be true, whether the other is or not. What is more, the relationship between the two statements raises crucial sociological issues: Why do people believe something for which there is no basis? How far does the belief that a particular social situation exists help to create it? The gap between these two types of statements constitutes Descartes's entire epistemological problem. What justification do we have for jumping from the content of 'my' consciousness to a world outside? On what grounds can we be assured that the ideas in our minds not only reflect a world outside but reflect it reasonably accurately?

The process of systematic doubt has led us to the conception of a pure, disembodied consciousness, for, so Descartes argues, consciousness cannot be dependent on our body if its existence can be demonstrated independently and prior to that of any body.[11] Belief in the priority and independence of mind is, of course, far from eccentric, being entrenched in Christian belief and in philosophic traditions going back to Plato, which is no doubt why Descartes so readily accepted an argument of doubtful force. After all, I can be sure of the existence of silk shirts without knowing about silkworms, but this does not mean that the former are independent of the latter.

Even if we accept that the mind is independent of the body and does not owe its existence to it, we still believe that it is related to the body, and through it to an external world. But since the insight which assured us of existence as conscious beings did not also guarantee us a body and a world around us, Descartes had to discover within the contents of his consciousness a foothold enabling him to climb out of this isolation and get back to assurance of an external world. He therefore took stock of the ideas he found in his mind.[12] There were, firstly, those which seemed to be thrust upon his mind and therefore, unless produced by an unconscious part of his mind, came from outside. Even so, this kind of idea may give a distorted picture of outside reality. The second kind of idea is those which we make up—unicorns, for example—or any technological invention. There remains, in Descartes's view, a third category of ideas, which cannot be accounted for either by experience or imagination. These he calls innate ideas, meaning not that we possess them at birth, but that they emerge within us as we mature; they are part of our endowment, just as the propensity to grow tall may be an innate characteristic though we are born tiny babies.

The particular idea which Descartes claims to be innate and singles out for discussion is that of God as the perfect being. It cannot derive from experience because we never encounter perfection. Without being perfect ourselves—and the doubt with which we start demonstrates our imperfection—and without any experience of perfection, we do not have the material to make up the idea of perfection.[13] We might think that we can extrapolate the idea of perfection from our experience of more or less perfect things, but Descartes claims that the boot is on the other foot: how could we judge something to be imperfect unless we had that inbuilt standard of perfection?

Once this inbuilt standard is granted, it follows that as nothing comes from nothing—a typical rationalist presupposition—there must be an adequate cause for our idea of perfection, and that can only be the actual existence of a perfect being.[14] Descartes adds the argument that this perfect being of which we have an idea must by definition exist, or it would not be perfect.[15] These and some of his other arguments do not strike modern readers as very convincing, and many philosophers have attacked them. Though there is no need to defend or to attack them here, the reader should beware of the idea that a man like Descartes was merely silly. It has been stressed against the second argument, derived from medieval philosphy, that existence is not a quality. I can form the idea of a perfect swimming pool, but the question whether it is there in my garden is quite separate. It would be futile for me to argue that a swimming pool would not be perfect unless I could actually walk out and plunge in. Descartes appreciated this as well as we do, but he saw God as special and unique, not one object among others but the ultimate reality on which everything else depends. To medieval man this idea was a self-evident and crucial certainty, and it was almost equally obvious to Descartes's contemporaries, which made the so-called ontological argument convincing. To us this way of thinking is no longer natural; it may help us to appreciate the argument if we make its underlying assumption explicit by using 'reality' for 'God'. The idea that reality is that which exists by definition sounds convincing even today.

Once we are satisfied that there is a God whose perfection would not allow him to deceive us, our doubts are stilled. The mind is seen to be part of an order which it can grasp. Errors may still occur, because we use our freedom to employ our faculties carelessly, fail to allow for distortions which are part of the order of things, or generally jump to conclusions when the evidence is insufficient.[16] But if we play our cards right, all knowledge is within our grasp. It is at this stage that we can reexamine the many beliefs that were pushed aside as questionable at the beginning of Descartes's investigation. They may now be readmitted, at least as plausible hypotheses, so it is reasonable to believe that we have bodies and live in a physically extended world which affects our senses in a multitude of ways.[17]

In the end this philosophic revolution did not produce such an upheaval in our ordinary beliefs. Philosophies usually do not. But the order of steps in the argument is significant and has had its effect on the intellectual life of our civilisation. Doubt, consciousness, God, the physical world, are the stepping stones. The first step signals the rejection of tradition and authority, the second asserts the priority of mind over body and the independence of the one from the other. That God should come before the external world is particularly significant. Common sense takes what we see and touch as more certain and real than what we think. But this is precisely where, according to Descartes, we have gone wrong. What we can think clearly is more certain than what we see. Only within the context of carefully tested thought can we establish the reliability of our senses.

This is the rationalism which characterises Descartes and his successors. Though we may smile at these excessive claims for reason, which seem shallow and overoptimistic, that is because, philosophically speaking, Descartes's argument did not go far enough in illuminating the relation between thinking and sensing and left obscurities to be eliminated by subsequent philosophers. For common sense the journey of discovery ends up too close to home to be wildly exciting.

Yet the student of society in particular should appreciate the significance of these developments for the life of that age when Christian fought Christian and heretics were burned. Humane and thoughtful people who longed for the end of conflict and persecution looked to reason as an arbiter. It was also needed to end the widespread belief in witches and possession by devils; all over Europe people were being persecuted, tortured, and killed on these grounds. Of course some people were more tolerant and humane than others; some more sceptical about the evidence that a particular person had made a pact with the devil, but as H. R. Trevor Roper has argued, it was only the rationalist revolution, heralded by Descartes, which cut at the root of the whole business.[18] In the light of reason and the strict epistemological criteria laid down by Descartes, the whole web of superstition came to look like the nonsense it is. He had no difficulty, either, in casually dismissing astrology, which was still taken quite seriously by distinguished and even scientifically minded contemporaries.

Today we have lost this buoyant confidence in the knowability of the universe and the capacity of the intellect to march undeviatingly towards its final illumination. Well into the nineteenth century distinguished thinkers and scientists believed that the completion of the edifice of knowledge was just round the corner, but we are more sceptical. Science now seems like fishing in an inexhaustible ocean rather than marching towards Camelot.

Yet in our scientific approach we have remained the heirs of Descartes, and the title *Discourse on Method* indicates what makes his work important. The knowledge which man acquires in daily life through familiarity, trial and error, or by being given the information and insights which mankind has used for survival from the dawn of its existence, becomes science through awareness and use of method. We must have agreed principles so that we can test claims to the possession of true knowledge and consider what kind of evidence is to be accepted as reliable and the conclusions it allows us to draw. More specific questions are linked to these general ones: How can we come by reliable evidence? How are we to arrange and use it? How can we test our conclusions, and how confident can we be when we have done so? What we call the scientific method is a particular set of answers to questions such as these. Methodology systematically reexamines and refines these answers; it leads into, and provides the framework for, considerations of technique, but is itself grounded in epistemology.

Science had its beginning in distant antiquity, long before Descartes, who was not the only pioneer of modern science or even the first in his own time. The theory of knowledge is not his invention, either, for the very early Greek philosophers asked epistemological questions. But no one has formulated the demand for an epistemologically grounded method more clearly, sharply, and dramatically. No one has made us more conscious of the constant need to ask, Do I really know this? Does my conviction really rest on sound, rationally acceptable evidence?

Cartesianism and the Methods of Social Research

In physical science the battle of method has been fought and won; no one will confuse what the householder knows about the coal in his grate with the scientific knowledge about carbons contained in physics or chemistry. But in sociology the issue is far from dead. One constantly encounters assertions which have not been critically examined and have no better justification than that they are widely believed. Techniques are used—questionnaires are an example—without examining what they provide evidence for; a person's saying that he will vote for X is not necessarily evidence that he will do so. In other cases, such as participant observation, one wonders what solid evidence is offered. For sometimes there is no sign that the investigator has any idea of what kind of evidence is needed to support a claim. A striking example of this occurred in *New Society* a few years ago, where an author condemns himself out of his own mouth: 'This article attempts to chart a profile of the coloured man's view (of the British). To piece it together I talked to thirty coloured people in and around London.'[19] One hardly needs to spell out to even an elementary student of sociology that two and a half dozen Londoners are less than an adequate sample of the coloured population of Britain. If some researchers are too bold, others are too timid. Some schools of sociology have retreated from whole areas of social life because they appear methodologically untractable. Here lessons can still be learned from Descartes's rigour and the élan with which he combined scepticism with intellectual boldness.

For Descartes, as for philosophers before and after him, mathematics fulfilled the requirements of precise rational knowledge; it was a model of what science should be. The introduction of mathematical reasoning and techniques (such as those Descartes himself had developed) into the sciences was, of course, an integral part of their signal success. Today statistical techniques are widely used to organise material and single out causal factors within the social sciences, and few would deny their importance. The use of statistics, however, depends on the possibility of isolating or abstracting quantifiable data. That this can be done successfully and to good purpose in the physical sphere is well established. It cannot be as obviously applied to thoughts and feelings.

It may not be possible to derive a clear, unambiguous programme for the social sciences from Descartes's epistemological stance, but from its ambiguities—which have proved productive in other spheres—two quite different positions, both pointing to him as unintentional progenitor, can be extrapolated. We may argue that the total otherness of consciousness from extended reality requires a completely distinct approach to the former, namely an introspective contemplation of the contents of consciousness leading to their critical examination. This I take to be the characteristic approach of phenomenology and its founder, Husserl, who himself associated it with the Cartesian approach. On the other hand Descartes is not entirely blameless for the development of behaviourism. Once we accept that the acquisition of precise knowledge depends on the use of the scientific methods so obviously successful in the physical sciences and also that the human body is a complex machine functioning according to mechanical laws like all other physical things, it is tempting to concentrate on the study and explanation of the way the human body behaves.

That Descartes's work has fathered such different, even diametrically opposed, lines of approach to the social sciences is part of his tremendous influence, but it also highlights the reason why that influence has been exposed to fundamental criticism. The crux of the matter is his conception of a disembodied consciousness, a pure thinking ego, only loosely connected to a dead physical universe that works according to mechanical laws. Plants and animals, and indeed the human body, are part of that physical world, are, in fact, machines. The idea of the psychophysical unity of the person in his individuality is lost and so is the sense that man's part of the environment and a fellow creature of the other animals. Emotions and moods appear merely irrational, reverence for tradition, for the products of historical growth, prejudice. Knowledge is increasingly seen as the source of power to manipulate the world. This point of view, rational, antihistorical and manipulative, has aided the triumph of science and technology. It encouraged the French Revolution, which enthroned reason in place of Christianity, and the Industrial Revolution, which established the machine in place of the craftsman. Impersonal bureaucratic organisations have taken the place of organic communities. This is the spirit of the modern world— our world—and it owes not a little to the inspiration of Cartesian philosophy.

What we think of this heritage depends on the personal view we take of the balance sheets of gains and losses. Better health and longer life, cheap consumer goods, fast travel and labour-saving devices, and the end of many prejudices and superstitions and of much religious persecution are examples of the benefits we have reaped. Wars of unprecedented destructiveness, the threat of even more terrible ones, the despoiling of nature and pollution, the destruction of entire animal species, and a sense of meaninglessness felt by some people are part of the other side of the coin. Certainly thinkers who have been particularly struck by the darker side of our civilisation, for example Kierkegaard and Nietzsche and the modern Existentialists, have placed some of the responsibility on the Cartesian influence. It may also be noted that, as R. A. Nisbet has forcefully argued, much of the development of sociology is closely related to the reaction against this Cartesian rationalism.[20]

Beyond noting the fact that Descartes's views were themselves instrumental in shaping social attitudes, we need not pursue and evaluate the practical consequences any further. The point that Descartes's dualism and rationalism turned people's minds towards physical rather than social science and produced a more adequate basis for the former than for the latter is clearly of much greater importance in this context. No less significant is that the encouragement this philosophy eventually gave to the study of man tended to produce somewhat one-sided developments such as behaviourism and phenomenology.

There is, however, an entirely different aspect of Descartes's dualism which requires careful consideration. However unsatisfactory the logical implications of it may be—and it has received some harsh treatment in modern philosophy, for example, from Gilbert Ryle[21]—it points to something important and fundamental. This is the fact that the natural attitude of common sense is best expressed by such a dualism.

My mind and my body are independent entities; I can think a thought to its logical conclusion, a process which does not appear to me manifestly determined by anything physical. Nor need I give any physical sign that the thought process is going on. It can remain hidden and accessible only to my introspection. In the same way physical processes which are neither conscious nor mind-controlled are going on in my body. Precisely because they are independent entities, mind and body can also interact; I can move my body because a thought process has led me to the decision to do so and am conscious of pain because my body has been bruised.

All the statements in the above paragraph represent, I believe, the kind of thing we want to say in everyday life when we are not under the spell of a particular 'philosophical' or scientific theory. They do raise, however, various philosophical questions. Why, for example, should the validity of my reasoning be independent of physical processes when interference with these processes (like the administration of drugs) can interfere with thought? And what is the value of accepting that there are private mental processes not accessible to anyone else, if they cannot be compared and assessed? The main difficulty is, however, to see how mind and body can interact. How one memory awakens another or how one thought follows logically on another seems intelligible enough, and we also feel that we can understand how nerves activate muscles and thus how an arm can lift an object. But there is something opaque about thought moving my limbs or an impact on my body being experienced as pain. Since Descartes's theory that this interaction takes place in the pineal gland does not really illuminate the problem and has been found plausible by few, philosophers who followed him have put forward theories which replace the concept of interaction. Spinoza's psychophysical parallelism is an example.

Yet we must come back to the point that interaction between body and mind is the commonsense assumption we all make in everyday life. For the sociologist this has a double significance; he cannot ignore the dualistic way in which human beings think about their own actions and interpret the situations in which they find themselves. People spank their children to improve their mental attitudes or give tasty meals to their friends to cheer them up. In their actions they are aware of purposes which they pursue and principles by which they live. The sociologist's description of the social scene can hardly ignore these purposes and principles or the mental effects which other people's behaviour and the impact of the external world is supposed to have. If he conducts a survey or listens to people as a participant observer, these are the kind of interpretations he will get and must try to understand and evaluate.

Equally significant is that sociologists' own generalisations and hypotheses constantly refer to the interaction between the physical and the mental sphere: the Protestant ethic affects modes of production, ideology influences voting behaviour, scarcity of essential commodities affects moral standards. There are correlations between birth rates and religious views about birth control. No one will be surprised to find theories like these in sociological literature.

To grasp the full methodological implications of the widespread belief that mental and physical events interact we must hold fast to the fundamental otherness of mind and body as postulated in Descartes' philosophy. It would be a mistake and falsify the whole issue to assume that we are merely correlating religious and sexual behaviour, moral actions and circumstances. We are talking of ideas on the one hand and physical occurrences on the other, and each must be tackled in a different way because they have different structural characteristics. For example, spatial and temporal continuity is an important criterion in the physical sphere but not in that of ideas; but thoughts, though not events, may either imply each other or be logically inconsistent.

While Cartesian dualism preserves the social world for us as we know it and as the sociologist has to study it, other philosophical points of view seem to distort the social world by making one or the other of its ingredients a dependent variable. Materialism degrades mental activity into shadowboxing; idealism transforms the physical world into a dream; psychophysical parallelism creates, as we shall see, particular paradoxes about choice; preestablished harmony postulates a script according to which the mental and the physicaal are coordinated through eternity. All these theories provide a rational framework for explaining human life, but Descartes's has the special merit of staying closest to common sense and, at a cost, pinpointing the real methodological problems we have to face. The very insistence on the otherness of mind makes its relation to the body opaque, but it is to Descartes' credit that he did not seek an escape in what has been called a 'ghost in the machine' conception.[22] As all readers of ghost stories know, that would mean that the soul or the mind can be observed by the senses and in turn may act on the physical world; the mind–body relation would in that case be explained by a form of refined behaviourism, that is, by the idea that the mind is just another but less substantial material. Descartes would have no truck with this. 'I am not', he says, 'something tenuously infused into that body; I am not a breath of air, nor a flame, nor vapour, nor breath itself, nothing of all that I can invent with my imagination' (by imagination he meant the use of images).[23]

The Beginnings of a Sociology of Knowledge

So much for the relevant points which can be extracted from what I am tempted to call Descartes's 'official' philosophy. But behind Cartesius, the pupil of the Jesuits who sought refuge in his quiet study and explored his own consciousness for rational proofs of God, we can discern another Descartes, a man of the world and an expert swordsman who sought to complete his education by travel and military service. This Descartes believed that the empirical study of the world around him—for example, the dissection of animals—was more relevant than book-learning. He believed in experiment,[24] in the pragmatic knowledge contained in crafts and practical skills of all kinds,[25] and in the technological application of science, and thus brought a hitherto neglected aspect of the philosophy of reason to the fore.

> For they [his notions concerning physics] caused me to see that it is possible to attain knowledge which is very useful in life, and that, instead of that speculative philosophy which is taught in the schools, we find a practical philosophy by means of which, knowing the force and the action of fire, water, air, the stars, the heavens and all other bodies that environ us, as distinctly as we know the different crafts of our artisans, we can in the same way employ them in all those uses to which they are adapted and thus render ourselves the masters and possessors of nature.[26]

This shrewd, down-to-earth observer of the world and human affairs commented from time to time on the problems of knowledge. These comments, which really belong to the sociology of knowledge, are interspersed in his works without always being fully integrated with their philosophic content. One pervasive theme is uncertainty. Descartes started his philosophical argument with systematic doubt, which served the purely theoretical purposes of laying bare the epistemological foundations of our beliefs, but he made it clear that such doubts do not touch our everyday life. We do not worry that our senses are constantly deceiving us, because they do so occasionally; we can easily distinguish waking from dreaming and do not suspect a cosmic conspiracy to deceive us. Only madmen doubt the solid existence of the objects around us. But I suggest that behind Descartes's elegant use of sceptical arguments lie more genuine worries about personal bias, cultural relativity, and prejudice as sources of uncertainty, confusion, and controversy. Here, one may argue, lies the emotional spring for his passionate quest for certainty.

This theme is introduced near the very beginning of the *Discourse*: 'We differ in opinion, not because some of us have a larger share of reason than others, but because we think in different ways, and do not fix our attention upon the same objects.'[27] Descartes believes this to be the reason for the deplorable state of philosophy to which he refers a few pages later, saying that 'it has been cultivated by the most excellent minds that have appeared in this world for many centuries past, and nevertheless, every one of its propositions is still subject to dispute.'[28] These unresolved differences of opinion have, according to him, further consequences for the whole state of knowledge. 'As for the other sciences', he continues, 'whose principles are borrowed from philosophy, I judged that nothing stable could have been built on such insecure foundations.'[29]

Descartes clearly has no intention of deriving a complete scepticism from his conviction that different and even conflicting conclusions are based on differing interests and modes of thought. He believes that there are more and less effective methods of inquiry and thought and that he has discovered the 'right method'. It would be hard to imagine what he thought he had accomplished, if it was not the discovery of the right method, that is, the cogent demonstration of how solid, indubitable truth could be achieved.

Nonetheless he makes a number of very interesting qualifications, and though it could be argued that these are rather a matter of courtesy than of conviction and that as an urbane man of the world he is careful not to bludgeon his readers by apparently arrogant claims, it is not safe to explain away the manifest meaning of statements carefully composed by a great thinker. For example, he introduces his method by saying, 'My good fortune led me in early youth into a certain course of thought opening up various considerations and principles, with the help of which I have formed a method designed, as I think, to provide me with what I require in order to increase my knowledge step by step.'[30] It is interesting to reflect upon what, in the light of other passages in the same text, he could mean by 'good fortune'. He explicitly denies that he has exceptional intellectual endowments,[31] and would have considered it presumptuous to attribute his achievement to divine inspiration. As he was critical of his education and the tradition in which it was steeped, his luck could not mean inspiration from a particular book or teacher. Nor was it a successful guess or a lucky hunch, for he insists— and this is a cornerstone of one of his crucial arguments for the existence of God—that everything, including ideas, must have an adequate cause.

Though Descartes does not expand on the nature of his own good fortune, he does have a number of things to say about the various factors which influence our opinions, one of these being our own biologically and environmentally determined makeup. For, Descartes argues, 'even the mind is so dependent on the temperament and the bodily organs that, if a way can be found of making men wiser and more skilful than they have so far proved, I believe we must look for it in medicine'.[32] So the discovery of truth appears to depend on health, diet, and regular habits and therefore (it is not farfetched to add) on food supplies, health service, and sanitation. He also notes that the mind can be biased in its thinking: 'We know how subject we are to error in what concerns us closely and how suspicious we should be of the judgments delivered by our friends, when they pronounce in our favour'.[33]

Even more interesting is the attention which Descartes gives to the social and cultural environment. Noting the differences between societies of different ages or different parts of the globe, he concludes that comparative studies can help us to judge our own society better and rid us of our prejudices about other people: 'It is good to know something about the manners and customs of other nations so that we may judge more sanely of our own, and may not think that whatever is contrary to our own mode of life is both ridiculous and unreasonable, as is usually the case with those who have seen nothing'.[34] This passage occurs in a discussion of the advantages and limitations of history and is not further expanded. However, he returns to the theme at the end of the section.

Thus the greatest benefit I derived from my observations was that, by noticing that many things which may seem to us quite extravagant and quite ridiculous are nevertheless commonly accepted with approval by other nations. I learned not to believe too firmly in what only custom and example had persuaded me to accept as true; and in this way, I freed myself, little by little, from many of the errors which obscure the natural light of the mind, and make us less capable of listening to reason.[35]

So he has learned from his comparison of civilisations—and note that he calls this the *greatest benefit* he derived from his observations—that opinions, and therefore practices, are culturally and socially determined. In other words, he has become aware that people think and act differently according to whether they have been brought up in France or China. This, he claimed, made him more tolerant of the customs of other nations and more sceptical of those of his own.

But once you abandon ethnocentric complacency, where does the process stop? On a superficial plane the point is obvious, trivial, and noncontroversial. Only a very stupid and ignorant middle-class Englishman will think it absolutely right to pick up peas with the back of his fork and consider other eating habits barbaric; it is not only manners, daily habits, and fashions that vary between different societies, but moral convictions and religious beliefs. Equally reasonable men may be Hindu or Muslim, Catholic or Lutheran according to where they were brought up. They may also be divided on the respective merits of different virtues. It is not unreasonable to assume that such matters were of vital concern to a man like Descartes and lent urgency to his epistemological inquiries. After all, the great journeys of discovery had brought an enlarged awareness of the world and its varied inhabitants, and the great schism in the church had reawakened concern about the grounds on which religious truth rested. It was only about three-quarters of a century before Descartes's birth that the earth was circumnavigated for the first time and that Luther pinned his thesis on the church door of Wittenberg.

It is tempting to argue that all this has nothing to do with knowledge, that on the contrary these are spheres Descartes contrasts to rational inquiry. On matters of mathematics or astronomy, he would assume, as do we, that Hindus and Christians, black men and white men, are still capable of a rational agreement. But in fact his own arguments have undermined such a solution. The demonstration of an omnipotent and all-good God who would not resort to deception is the linchpin of his whole philosophy and rests on his belief that we have an innate idea of perfection. The conviction that all religious and moral beliefs are culturally determined thus undermines the foundations of knowledge more radically than any of the traditional arguments of scepticism.

Therefore, to rescue objectivity, Descartes had to maintain—and this is part of rationalism—that some religious content, such as belief in a single omnipotent and all-good God, and some moral tenets, such as the goodness of truthfulness, were rationally grounded. It would follow that a rational core, common to different religions and moral codes, could be distinguished from the culturally determined spelling out of these creeds and codes. But this clearly raises further difficulties. Can we really convict the intelligent polytheist of irrationality and claim that Christianity is superior to other religions because it alone rests on rational grounds? Even if we had settled these questions and satisfied ourselves that Western man had used his reason to better purpose than men of other civilisations and was also the recipient of the only true revelation, we would still—on Descartes's own premises—have to account for this 'good fortune'.

He certainly did not think through and make explicit the implications of his sociology of knowledge and may not have done so from worldly prudence, for he was anxious, as we know, to be left in peace and not run into conflict with the secular or religious authorities. He may have been unable or unwilling to press a line of argument that ran counter to deeply implanted convictions; nevertheless he must be given credit for widening the scope of rational inquiry by conjuring up the outline of a sociology of knowledge and hinting at some of the epistemological problems which it raises.

There is evidence that Descartes had a shrewd idea of the vast uncertainties he was raising. The way he talks about his own religion and morality is hardly that of a simpleminded Christian with unquestioning faith in the teaching of the Bible. It is true that he describes his view as provisionally adopted before the completion of his philosophy, but one may ask why he should communicate it in detail well after he had completed his philosophic system. His first maxim, he says, was to obey the laws and customs of my country, adhering to the religion in which God had given me the grace to be instructed since childhood, and governing myself in everything in accordance with the most moderate opinions . . . so commonly accepted in practice by the most sensible of those among whom I should have to live. . . . There may, it is true, be people just as sensible among the Persians and the Chinese as among us, but I thought it more expedient to regulate my behaviour according to those with whom I should have to live. And I also thought that in order to know their real sentiments, I should observe their actions rather than their words, not only because the corruption of our manners and customs makes most people unwilling to declare what they believe, but because many do not know it themselves; for the activity of thought by which we believe something is different from the activity by which we know we believe, so that the one can exist without the other.[36]

Nothing could be more sensible, yet it is astonishing that he makes no pretence of being under an unconditional obligation to obey the precepts of Christ. He will act in a particular way because he happens to have been brought up and live in a particular country—and even that in 'moderation'. His intention to follow common practice rather than official doctrine is even more striking, for here we have something like a behaviourist manifesto from the apostle of 'I think, therefore I am'. He would, of course, have been the last to deny the existence of consciousness, as some behaviourists seem to have done, but agrees with the methodological advantage of observing behaviour because of the difficulty of analysing and communicating the contents of consciousness.

Here, in a nutshell, is virtually the whole case frequently made since Descartes's time against questionnaires and interviews. People may lie or dissemble; they may not know their own minds. The distinction made between a belief which expresses itself in our attitudes and actions and an articulate consciousness of the belief also points forward to theories about the unconscious or subconscious and the conception of 'bad faith' in Marxist and Existentialist literature.

Descartes's underlying scepticism also found expression in his appeal to pragmatic criteria:

It seemed to me that I should find more

truth in the reasonings which a man makes with regards to matters which touch him closely, and of which the outcome must be to his detriment, if his judgment has been at fault, than in the reasonings of a man of learning in his study, whose speculations remain without effect, and are of no further consequence to him than that he may derive all the more vanity from them the further removed they are from good sense, because of the greater skill and ingenuity he has to employ to make them plausible.[37]

Ingenious armchair speculation is unreliable because subject to emotional bias. Theories may only be relied on when they have been exposed to the practical test of success or failure. It is not the 'scientific' meterologist but the sailor or fisherman who is worth listening to when he predicts storm or calm. The former will confidently predict, then calmly explain away the unforeseen outcome, and confidently predict again. The latter will not survive his errors for long. He must back his judgement with life and limbs, so his survival is a testimony to the accuracy of his views.

So for Descartes knowledge is what works in the practical affairs of men, just as it is the basis of the craftsman's skill. It is knowledge which gives man power over his environment, an idea taken up by subsequent philosophy (for example, pragmatism) which today seems neither surprising nor implausible. To remember these aspects of Descartes' thought helps us to correct any too narrowly drawn picture of him as an orthodox patron saint of rationalism.

I have specifically assembled these scattered passages because they show that Descartes was in deadly earnest about the scepticism which emerged from his psychological and sociological reflections about the basis of knowledge. Themes which have come to be associated with historicism (such as that of Marx), with psychoanalysis, and with modern sociologies of knowledge are clearly anticipated in his work.

Quite apart from the intrinsic interest and obvious relevance these Cartesian ideas have for current discussions of behaviourism, the techniques of social surveys, the testing of hypotheses in the social sciences, and the cultural determinants of science, they also throw further light on his whole conception of method. It is a historical mistake to think of seventeenth-century rationalism as naïvely confident of reason because blithely unaware of the strength of passions, the forces of social conditions, and the weight of tradition. It was not left to Romanticism and the historical schools of the nineteenth century to discover the forces which it was their virtue to emphasize.

On the contrary, it may be argued that emotional bias and social or historical relativity were clearly conceived as problems which the rational, scientific method was designed to solve. If we push the sceptical arguments, either the traditional ones of philosophy, or those which arise from psychological, sociological, or historical perspectives, to their limits, we must abandon all thought of knowledge of either the physical or the social world. By toying too dangerously with some of these doubts Descartes involved himself in inconsistencies, but if the concept of knowledge is to retain its meaning, we must agree with the essential conclusion with which he emerged from his uncertainties: that if we take proper care, our reason is capable of analysing and dissecting, thinking and calculating correctly and thus reaching true conclusions; taking proper care means using our capacity for inspecting these thought processes critically. At the same time he fully recognised that if thought is not to lose itself in a labyrinth of its own or fall prey to the distortions to which it is liable, it must be constantly tested against experience. The crunch comes when theories are tried out to see if they work. This is the essence of scientific method.

How thought and experience divide the task of acquiring knowledge between them and how they cooperate in the act of cognition is not adequately analysed in Descartes's work. Nor are we given sufficient grounds for rejecting scepticism in favour of the position he adopts. These were matters which subsequent philosophy had to take up.

4 . *Spinoza*: The Rational Order of Reality

No one has preached the gospel of reason more purely and consistently and lived it more heroically than Spinoza. His great contribution to our philosophic heritage, his boldly and cogently sketched picture of reality as a unitary and rationally structured system, provides a cornerstone of the philosophy of reason. It justifies our aspirations towards and confidence in comprehensive knowledge. His thought has exercised an enormous influence on subsequent philosophy as well as on European thought at large. Among the philosophers indebted to him Hegel is probably the most important, because he in turn exercised such an extensive influence on, among other theorists, Marx; and among poets, Goethe, Coleridge, Wordsworth, and Shelley.

In his own time his reputation spread slowly and remained controversial. He lived (1632–1677) in a time of savage religious wars when heretics were persecuted and witches burned, and thoughtful men turned to reason as the only possible arbiter between fanatical warring factions. Thus the Age of Reason, which to us, the distant heirs of its triumphs and calamities, seems a little smug and overoptimistic, was born in the face of chaos and violence. Spinoza shared with other outstanding representatives of this age—Descartes, Leibniz, and their successors like Wolf and Kant—this commitment to reason, but he differed from them in being much more detached from the civilisation and the traditions which were being reassessed. While all the others were brought up as Christians and continued to profess

Christianity, Spinoza was a Jew, descended from a family which had fled from the Spanish Inquisition and settled in Holland. By the time he was twenty–four he had rejected the Orthodox Jewish upbringing he had received and was solemnly excommunicated and expelled from the Jewish community as a dangerous freethinker. He never joined another religious association.

Spinoza remained similarly detached from social and economic life, because he sought neither wealth nor position, scorning to accept his patrimony and dissuading a friend from making him his main heir. He even rejected a pension offered by Louis XIV on condition that he dedicate a book to the monarch and turned down a professorship at Heidelberg University, partly because he wanted peace for his own philosophising and partly because, in the words of his letter or rejection, he 'did not know within what precise limits . . . the liberty of philosophising would have to be restrained so that it would not seem to interfere with the established religion of the principality'. Instead he was content to earn a very modest living by polishing lenses, at which he had developed a high degree of scientific skill.

However, far from being a prickly recluse, he enjoyed a circle of friends and acquaintances whom he met or with whom he corresponded extensively and which included distinguished scientists and the secretary of the newly founded Royal Society. Contemporary accounts agree that his dignity and natural grace charmed all who came in contact with him. Though he cultivated friendships, he sought fame as little as he sought wealth or social status. His first work was published anonymously, and his great main work remained in his desk for publication after his death. He was content to be an outsider, because he was convinced that reason was on his side. He felt himself at the centre of things from which his contemporaries had exiled themselves by their folly. This may sound confident to the point of arrogance, but with the hindsight of history we may think twice before judging him wrong. Certainly his calmness in the face of all adversity and the cheerfulness with which he approached his death from tuberculosis at the age of forty-five testify to his having found 'the road to blessedness' which his writings signpost.

As he undoubtedly spent his time speculating in a garret, he was, if anybody could ever be described in this way, an armchair theoretician. Yet one must beware of thinking that the theories of such a man are not based on, and have no relevance for, human experience. Every man, even one in the proverbial ivory tower, is a human being involved with other human beings and with the world around him. Everyone has been brought up in a family, must go shopping, and depends on various services, must tread the ground and handle different materials. Add to this that Spinoza read widely, learned about scientific advances and experimental procedures from his correspondence, and observed his immediate environment closely (there is a record, for instance, of his intense interest in a fight between spiders). What is more important, though, and often not sufficiently appreciated, is the intellectual penetration and imaginative power a man brings to his experience, for this enables him to transform meaningless titbits into enlightening experience. Men like Spinoza or Kant more than compensate for their relatively narrow experience by bringing an acute intelligence and a thoughtfully prepared conceptual framework to bear on it. They may, therefore, discover more about human nature and human relations than less well-endowed investigators who have roamed far and wide gathering mountains of information.

Spinoza's shrewd power of observation and practical judgment is evident in one of his asides, which coming from a bachelor much occupied with contemplating eternal verities, may strike the reader as remarkably perceptive: 'boys or youths, unable to endure with equanimity the rebukes of their parents, fly to the army, choosing the discomforts of war and the rule of a tyrant rather than the comforts of home and the admonishments of a father, suffering all kinds of burdens to be imposed upon them in order that they may revenge themselves upon their parents.[1] Another passage illustrates his alertness to social issues, his lively awareness of the world around him, combined with his philosophic presuppositions, led him to anticipate the need for a welfare state: 'to assist every one who is needy far surpasses the strength or profit of a private person. . . . The care, therefore, of the poor is incumbent on the whole of a society and concerns only the general profit.'[2]

Spinoza's theoretical speculations are more substantial, original, and interesting than his incidental observations and practical suggestions. It is well to remember, though, that one of the world's greatest metaphysicians had his feet very solidly planted on the ground.

God or Nature

Spinoza's *Ethic* starts with an issue as remote from sociology as it could possibly be: the nature of God. But if we are to appreciate how he changed our intellectual climate and prepared the ground for significant sociological developments, we must follow the lines of his argument. The title clearly indicates that the book is about the way man should live, so we are entitled to expect discussions of man's nature and of his involvement with other people in society; we are not disappointed. It is, however, the characteristic feature of the *Ethic*, the feature which makes it such a great book, that the discussion about human conduct is embedded in the widest possible context, which is the nature of reality and our power of knowing it. If Spinoza starts with God, it does not mean that the *Ethic* is a theological tract. To consider the nature of God is his highly original way of spelling out the nature of a world assumed to be intelligible.[3]

From the outset Spinoza parts company with Jewish and Christian monotheism by identifying God with the whole of reality, a point which he stresses throughout by the recurring phrase 'God or nature'. This identification contains—quite deliberately, one suspects—an ambiguity, or two-sidedness, which is an integral part of his whole philosophy. It means, on the one hand, that everything is divine and thus expresses a religious dedication (this justifies the description of Spinoza as 'god-intoxicated'). On the other hand it means that god is nothing except the reality which we experience, in a fragmented way, it is true, in everyday life and which we study in science. There is no way of turning from nature to nature's creator. This looked to some people like a trick to make irreligion respectable. Why call nature God? For it is not nature which Jews and Christians normally worship.

However, Spinoza was not arbitrary in his interpretation of the divine but genuinely tried to pinpoint fundamental issues hidden in the depth of religious thought and language. To this issue, as to everything else he touched, he brought the ruthless logic of a man wholly dedicated to reason. His point of departure can be easily spelled out. Throughout the ages people have talked about God in two different and, as he argued, inconsistent ways. God has been called perfect, infinite, omnipresent, all-powerful and all-knowing; he has been thought of as ultimate reality and the fountainhead of all being, but he has also been described as a person, more specifically as a king, father, or shepherd and given such human characteristics as the tendency to love, to be angry, or to be jealous. Even God's bodily attributes, such as having a face or hands, were frequently mentioned. These two sets of characteristics do not go together, and to talk as if they did was, in Spinoza's view, sheer confusion. How can an infinite being have face or hands? What can it mean for an omnipotent God to exercise his will or for ultimate reality to be jealous? Once we firmly grasp the true nature and function of religion, we have no trouble in deciding that the first set of characteristics is the one which truly describes the divine. Religion is not about placating someone in the world who is bigger and stronger than we are, but about coming to terms with the whole universe of which we are, irrevocably, part. Thinking of God as something like a human being is only a cosy anthropomorphism which corresponds to nothing in reality and can at best serve as a metaphor to help the simpleminded.

Spinoza's pantheism, his belief in an all-pervasive and impersonal God, was not new (though somewhat heretical in the Europe of his time). What was original and claims our special attention is the rigour of the arguments with which he developed his concept of God and drew out its implications. A God identical with the whole of reality meets the most important requirements of traditional theology: he is infinite, because there can be nothing which is outside him to limit him; he is omnipotent, because there can be no power outside him; he is free, because nothing can compel him; he is the source of everything and the whole of which everything is a part. The connection between God and man is therefore intellectually and morally misconceived if we think of it as a relation between two entities, however unequal. It must, instead, be conceived as the relation between the totality of things and the parts which make it up. This distinction, and not any particular qualities, makes for the total otherness of the divine. Thus all the characteristics with which we are familiar from the world of things can be attributed to God only in a sharply qualified form. God thinks in the sense that he is all thought, but not in the sense that he passes from proposition to proposition. His will cannot be a resolve to achieve something by effort, for what could a perfect and omnipotent being want, and what obstacles could he encounter? Instead God's will is his actual power expressed in the laws of nature. God does not feel love or anger, because he is not a person; yet there is love, anger, and the rest in him because persons are part of the encompassing reality of God. Though there is no one to respond to our prayers, reality will sustain us if by such means as scientific knowledge we achieve the right relation to it.

These paradoxes are not part of the ineffable mystery of the divine. Nothing could be further from the mind of a rationalist like Spinoza than to entertain the possibility that something is inexplicable in principle. The difficulties stem from the problem of using terms coined to describe particular things, to refer to a larger whole of which they are parts. This is a problem familiar to sociologists, for it arises—though not so radically—when we talk of any group or collective. A football club, let us say, confronts the individual player as a single entity he must deal with; it is his employer, for example, with whom he has his contract. Yet, strictly speaking, the club has no separate existence apart from the players, managers, or financial backers which make it up. Even on this mundane level, paradoxes therefore arise. A football club cannot play football because a club is not the kind of being which has feet to kick a ball, yet it does play football in the sense that the players of which it consists do. Underlying Spinoza's discussion of God there is a penetrating examination of the relationship between parts and wholes of considerable interest to sociologists.[4]

Relating ourselves to the whole of which we are part is, for Spinoza, a matter of personal salvation, the true subject of all religion. Because the most appropriate and effective form this relationship to God can take is that of rationally knowing the whole and the part we play in it, the primary task, which Spinoza accomplishes in his analysis of the divine nature, is to map out a conceptual framework. When he talks about God he is also talking about the presuppositions of science. His insistence on the unity of reality and the inseparability of God from his creation can thus be recognised as a prerequisite of all, including scientific, rational knowledge.

It is easy to see that alternative conceptions make the world incomprehensible. If, as many religions maintain, there is a God who is separate from his creation but occasionally interferes with it, then it becomes impossible to know things accurately, explain them convincingly, or derive predictions from them. If litmus paper changes its colour in an experiment, does this mean that acid is present? Not necessarily: it could be a miracle. Similarly a man's action may be due to his mental makeup and social circumstances, or he may be inspired by God and the consequences of his effort transformed by divine intervention. Nature would remain shrouded in mystery, and so would the nature of God. Experience of the world could not give us any indication of the divine, because the word would be ambiguous and unable to reflect the thoughts and intentions of its maker; otherwise he would not have to interfere with it.

If, however, as Spinoza maintains, God is identical with his creation (because an infinite being leaves no room for anything outside itself, an omnipotent one can allow for no unrealised potentialities, and an omniscient one could not have slipped up and need to do remedial tinkering), then nature is God and its laws are God's will. We can aspire towards a unified system of knowledge which is as much knowledge of God as of nature.

Once theology is assimilated to science, reality becomes fully accessible to reason. This is the claim which Spinoza confidently put forward and which made the linchpin of his arguments. In practice we, as limited beings, are condemned to have only partial knowledge, but in principle we can know anything. Once we appreciate this basic premise, we have a key to much in Spinoza that seems arbitrary to modern readers. On the first page of the *Ethics* they are confronted by a number of definitions and axioms from which in subsequent pages the nature of God is deduced. To the questions why he produced these particular definitions and how he arrived at them, Spinoza gives no explicit answer. But there is one: these definitions and the deductions from them spell out what reality must be like if it is to be know-able by a rational mind.

Spinoza certainly believed that we are capable of knowing the world. Unlike Descartes, he rejected systematic doubt as a pos-sible starting point, because he recognised that once we give full reign to scepticism there is no road back to certainty, and we must throw in our hands and despair of both science and phi-losophy. Knowledge, he argued, carried its own hallmark; truth shone by its own light. 'A person who knows anything', he wrote, 'by that very fact knows that he knows'.[5] It is hard to see how we can avoid agreeing with this. If I am unsure whether I have done my sum correctly or not, for obviously people do make mistakes, I can do it again and make sure that I have done so with care, for there is no process other than adding (or some equivalent manipulation of figures) by which we can check an addition. So, instead of starting by asking if I really know what I think I know, or see what I think I see, the *Ethics* revolves around the question of what reality must be like for me to know what I do know or will be able to learn in the future. Spinoza's answer spells out the rationalist postulate that a rational order of reality must correspond to man's rational power of cognition, by mapping out the divine nature, which is also substance, na-ture, or the universe.

From this initial stipulation Spinoza deduces specific features of reality. If reality is a single intelligible system, mind and matter cannot be two separate but interacting parts of reality.[6] The argument against this possibility is similar to the one against God and nature being separate but interacting entities. If a phys-iologist studying brain or nerve processes has to allow for the possibility that thought processes set off or interfere with phys-iological events, he can never produce reliable physiological ex-planations. It is equally impossible to explain how one thought gives rise to another if they are the sole product of a physical process. To avoid this pitfall, the two spheres of mind and matter must therefore be treated as two separate, but equally valid and equally comprehensive ways of describing reality. Conceived in terms of matter, reality is the totality of extended nature (what today we might call the space continuum). Conceived as mind, it is the totality of all possible knowledge. We shall see presently how Spinoza explained apparent interaction in these terms. The methodological conclusions he drew are particularly interesting.

Individual objects—tables or human bodies—are, for Spinoza, modes or modifications of the space continuum, configurations which reality assumes in particular places and at specific times. Mental activites are, correspondingly, configurations of ideas. Individual plants or persons within nature are like the ripples or waves on the ocean which for a time assume individual shapes and identities without ceasing to be part of the sea.

To be knowable, Spinoza concluded, reality must be causally ordered and determined in every respect.[7] Given that order, what existed did so necessarily ad what did not, could not exist. If the ground has the right properties, is dug and manured in the right way, and receives certain seeds and a specified amount of sun and rain, it is inevitable that a certain flower will grow. Given other conditions, it is impossible. What we call 'contingent' is something which does not exist from the necessity of its own nature, but which is still necessary in the context of nature. There is nothing about a buttercup which compels it to exist, but given a whole set of circumstances, it must.

Liberty, in this strictly ordered universe, means being self-determined or determined from within.[8] As everything is interdependent in the structure of the universe, only God or nature can, strictly speaking, be described as free, because determined by its own laws. But Spinoza considered that man can be relatively free, to the extent to which his own thoughts determine his actions. This view of freedom has, like most others, an air of paradox, because it allows no scope for spontaneity; yet it is also plausible, for surely freedom must mean being able to do what we want to do, what our own natural impulses or reflections incline us to (and not what we have no motive for). I want to be free to eat when I am hungry, not when I have no interest in food. The case can be made even more convincingly in terms of political freedom: a free country is not one of complete lawlessness, but one in which the laws governing it are made by the citizens. Such a theory, allowing that free actions are explainable and predictable, chimes in well with the sociologist's concerns. It becomes arguable and has, indeed, been argued by sociologists like Max Weber, that the freer the action—the more, that is, that it flows from the agent's own nature and is based on deliberate and rational choice—the more easily it can be understood and anticipated.[9]

To his picture of a universe governed by general laws Spinoza added a qualification which has a direct bearing on sociology. These universal laws apply only to things which are genuinely alike because they share basic characteristics; they must not be confused with the generalisations we habitually make on the basis of commonsense classifications.[10] Rejecting a tradition derived from Plato and Aristotle, Spinoza was sceptical of the amount of knowledge contained in the definitions of such class concepts as 'tree' or 'horse'. They and the generalisations based on them are only rough approximations which serve as crutches for minds of limited power. Human beings cannot appreciate, let alone remember, every individual horse in all its uniqueness, so we superimpose images on each other until we have a general but fuzzy and inaccurate picture of 'the horse'. The student of sociology will recognise here the description of the characteristics and dangers of a stereotype. It is sometimes not easy to avoid talking about Jews, students, workers, teenagers, and the like, but we must remember how frequently these terms cover prejudices and misconceptions and, even at best, can be misleading when applied to individuals.

Something more is required, though, if a universe governed by general laws but containing no neat classes of objects is to become intelligible. The specific structure which Spinoza attributes to reality is highly characteristic of his whole approach; it has fruitful methodological implications and is of special interest, as we shall see, to the sociologist. Spinoza makes a point largely neglected by philosophies of science, which tend to concentrate on general laws, by stressing that reality is an individual consisting of individuals.[11] Today we might say that it is a system of systems.

An ingenious and useful definition of individuality provides the cornerstone of this approach: 'By individual things I understand things which are finite and which have a determinate existence; and if a number of individuals so unite in one action that they are all simultaneously the cause of one effect, I consider them all so far as one individual thing.'[12] What is so ingenious about this definition is that by giving a clear operational criterion, it avoids all metaphysical controversy about the nature of individuality. Students of sociology will have come across discussions concerning whether nations, societies, or other groups can be described as individuals and whether explanations in terms of such entities are sufficiently basic or ought to be translated into accounts which refer to only one type of individual, namely individual human beings.[13] Of course, it depends on what you mean by 'an individal', and Spinoza's definition makes this crystal clear. A football team, for example, is an individual insofar as it competes with other teams. The effect of beating another team can only be attributed to it and to no other individual, such as a particular player. Obviously the individual team consists of individual players, one of whom took the first free kick or scored the last goal. When that player goes home he is part of another complex individual—the noisy family which is a nuisance to the neighbours, or the branch of the Rotary Club which supports local charities. In each case the relationship between an individual and the larger individual to which he belongs is governed by certain principles or rules (and this is why it is legitimate to translate Spinoza's concept of 'individual' by that of 'system').

This relationship between systems and their parts can be extended upwards and downwards. A player's hand, let us say, has a structure of its own and can be seen as an individual which produces its own distinct effects. A free kick is ordered because a player's *hand* touched the ball. The football team—to move in the other direction—is part of a club and that club is part of a league which, by having its own activity, such as organising football competitions, fulfills the definition of being an individual. Thus we can talk about individuals which are not persons without creating any mystery.

Reality, or God, is the individual which contains the hierarchies of all other individuals and so is the system of all systems. Within it everything has its place in an order of overlapping contexts, and this place defines its nature. This whole conception also accounts for apparent paradoxes about change and permanence. Just as a football league has not changed because a particular player has been transferred, and is not in motion though there are players running about on various football grounds, so

God remains unchanging and at rest though there is change and movement throughout the universe. Presently we shall return to the bearing all this has on Spinoza's theory of knowledge and, through that theory, on the methodology of the social sciences.

Man and His Passions

From his general conception of reality Spinoza derived a distinctive, detailed, and highly original conception of man which is relevant for students of the human world who must presuppose a general picture of human nature in their empirical research. They must have an idea of what they are looking for and how it may reveal itself. Spinoza used his theory that mind and matter are alternative ways of looking at reality to solve familiar but vexing problems about the relations between body and mind which Descartes' conception of the two as separate but interacting substances had left obscure. True, Descartes' view appears to reflect common sense. I raise my arm because the idea of doing so has entered my mind; I feel disgruntled because I have a cold. But this two-way traffic, so Spinoza insists, remains unintelligible, and any explanation in terms of it is unilluminating. It remains far from obvious how bodily movement can create or alter an idea, and how thought can precipitate physical change.

Rejecting the idea that we can reduce one of these spheres to the other, treating mental phenomena as mere by-products of physical ones (as materialists do) or physical occurrences as the contents of mental activity (as idealists do),[14] Spinoza treated mind and body as two sides, or two aspects, of a single reality, two ways of viewing a person. The mind is simply the idea of the body, much as the concept 'table' is the idea of a physical table.[15] Because these are two ways of apprehending the same reality, they must always be in step; thus Spinoza arrives at what has come to be called a theory of psychophysical parallelism. Strictly speaking, since there is only one reality presenting itself to us under different aspects, there can be no interaction.[16] Brain activity does not cause me to think, nor can I precipitate changes in the brain by starting to think. The two go together.[17] I cannot think even for a fraction of a second without something going on in my brain, and there can be no process in the brain which is not reflected in some way or other in my consciousness. To say that I feel excited *because* I took a stimulating drug or that my pulses are racing *because* I feel anxious is only a confusingly short-circuited explanation. The drug speeds my heartbeat, and this must present itself as excitement in consciousness, just as my state of anxiety causes other feelings and thoughts which have their physiological counterparts. To explain anything usefully we must link physical causes with physical effect and mental causes with mental effect, because changing your frame of reference in the middle of an explanation can never be useful. Though the theory that bodily and mental events are ultimately identical and that descriptions of them in one or the other form are equivalent may not be immediately palatable to common sense, there is some common sense evidence to support it. We all know that a man who feels anxious and whose pulse is racing may be soothed either by talking to him or by giving him a sedative. The chat, as it soothes his mind, will also slow his pulse; the pill, as it affects his pulse, will expel his anxieties. It is hard to imagine the one being achieved without the other.

Spinoza's next move in sketching his image of man was to devise a dynamic theory of mental processes. Modelling his theory on the successful approach of disciplines like physics or chemistry, he tried to explain the workings of the mind in terms of a few basic factors. The first and most important of these he called the 'conatus', which he defined as a universal force not confined to man (he was, after all, determined to treat man as only one among the objects of nature).[18] Basically the conatus is the tendency for anything to retain its essential nature or normal motion, to attain it if inhibited, or return to it if deflected. It is characteristic of a stone to be hard, and this presents itself as the stone's resistance to being squeezed or pulverised. In moving bodies the conatus is the tendency to continue in movement unless hindered. In man, as in all living creatures, the conatus is the drive for self-preservation and self-realisation (that is, the enhancement or enrichment of existence).

The second basic feature of man's psychology is that success in self-preservation, enlargement of self, and increase of power is accompanied by satisfaction, pleasure, joy, and similar positive emotions.[19] Frustration of the conatus, on the other hand, gives rise to displeasure, pain, and misery. Thus pleasurable states are a sure sign of successful self-assertion and power, painful ones of failure and impotence.

The third feature crucial for Spinoza's psychology is the mechanism which links the conatus and its success or frustration with love and hate.[20] Rigorous definitions specify how these states originate and what they consist of. If we associate pleasure with an object because we consider it the cause of that pleasure, we love that object, which means that we want to preserve it and keep it near us. If we associate suffering with an object which we think caused it, we hate it and want to destroy or, at least, remove it.

Because the human mind necessarily functions in these ways, they represent basic laws in terms of which all mental phenomena can be explained. It follows that people cannot change themselves—become more loving, more content, or more reasonable—by an effort of will, nor can they be changed by exhortations to pull themselves together or be more unselfish. People can only change themselves, or be changed by the influence of others, if the laws of human nature are applied to that purpose.[21] In other words, human nature functions and can be affected like any other part of nature. No persuasion and no effort of will can make a heavy object defy the law of gravity, but heavy aeroplanes can fly because they have been constructed in accordance with the laws of nature.

Once Spinoza had defined man as a psychophysical unit and described the basic principles according to which man's mind worked, he was ready to show how man could achieve freedom by gaining mastery of his passions. This not only rounds off his conception of human nature but also provides the crux of an argument which was designed to point out the 'road to blessedness', by showing how man can achieve the 'good life'. Before we can turn to Spinoza's view on the control of the passions, a little must be said about the way he defined good and bad.

Because reality is divine, it is perfect, and every part of it participates in this perfection, being more or less perfect according to its place in the whole and the power it can exercise.[22] Distinctions between good and bad can therefore have no objective validity, but they do have a proper place in judgements made from the point of view of a creature in the universe.[23] As human beings we can legitimately judge that certain things, like nourishing food or agreeably smelling flowers, are good for us whereas others, like some bacteria, are bad. But bacteria have their own perfection: they were as beautifully and rationally designed as the starry sky. They also have their own point of view; for them, no doubt, antibiotics are bad. What is bad for man may be good for streptococci. Spinoza's main point is to warn us against the arrogance of an anthropocentric view of reality. Reality is no less perfect for containing things detrimental to man. Good always means good for someone. A man calls what gives him pleasure good, because this indicates that it increases his power, and he will therefore love it. What causes him suffering, implying a loss of power, he considers bad and will hate.[24] The former he will naturally and 'by the highest right of nature' wish to maintain, the latter to destroy.[25] At first glance this looks like a theory of naked, ruthless self-interest, and indeed Spinoza believes that it would be futile and hypocritical to urge people to act against their true interest. However, his conception of what a human being's true interest is, seriously modifies the original harshness of the theory. Because it involves man's nature and relation to his fellows, this definition of man's true interest is highly significant for sociology.

Underlying Spinoza's definition of true interest is one of the central assumptions of the philosophy of reason, namely that man truly fulfills himself in the exercise of reason.[26] The mind's essential nature is to think and to know, so the more we engage in these activities the more powerful and therefore more happy we become. Knowledge is power in this direct sense but also, of course, in the sense of making us more efficient in dealing with our environment. Knowledge, not prayer, is the means of adjusting to reality and making it amenable.

It also follows that the life of reason unites us in mutual interdependence while passions and cravings divide us.[27] Several men in love with the same woman, or communities competing for resources in short supply, will be in conflict, for the success of one will deprive the others. It is not so with the life of reason and the pursuit of knowledge. It is no advantage to me as a student of physics that no one else is interested in the subject;

on the contrary it hinders me. I am better off if I can share my
interest with others and am surrounded by knowledgeable people. The pursuit of knowledge means cooperating in research,
making books available, and many other things which presuppose an ordered communal life. Thus once we recognise that
knowledge is an essential goal, we can also appreciate that ordered social life is not an optional way of living (to which we
may prefer the solitary life of a hermit, or the exclusiveness of
a group opting out of society), but an essential prerequisite which
we should accept even if less than perfect.[28]

Ultimately the individual's genuine interest lies in the soli-
darity of mankind. It is intelligent self-interest, and not some
abstract principle demanding self-sacrifice, which prompts moral
actions such as treating others justly, helping the poor, and
exercising self-restraint. Immorality is merely folly and short-
sightedness in the pursuit of one's interests.

It should also be remembered that for Spinoza the effort to
achieve a life of reason cannot be an ascetic, purely intellectual
goal; because body and mind are always in step, the efficient
functioning of the mind must coincide with the healthy and
active life of the body.[29] The necessary physical counterpart of
acquiring knowledge is the working of the brain and the capacity
of the body to see, hear, and move around so as to widen its
opportunities for stimulation by the environment. Furthermore,
because increase in power—whether seen in mental or physical
terms—is pleasurable, Spinoza's is a philosophy of enjoyment,
and he eloquently recommends enjoyment of food and drink,
flowers, ornaments, the theatre and music, and in fact 'all things
of this kind which one man can enjoy without hurting another'.[30]
Spinoza is a living refutation of the widespread opinion that
philosophy tends towards the dismal. For him the wise and good
man is happy, and the happiness testifies to his wisdom and
goodness.

To understand more fully how Spinoza envisaged life according to reason, we must look at his picture of the human situation.
Man is embedded in nature and is a small part of it constantly
exposed to the pulls and pressures of other parts which, at least
in combination, are always more powerful than he is.[31] Man's
subjection to these external forces—his liability to disease, his

need for food, his dependence on warmth—is reflected in his desires and emotions, which Spinoza called 'passions'. By this he meant not merely such states of infatuation as we mean by the term, but any state of being passively determined from outside.[32] When man is passive in this sense he is unfree or 'in bondage'. Self-realisation, liberation, salvation, or 'the road to blessedness' as he called it, lies in bringing these passions under the control of reason or, more precisely, replacing them by rational action.[33] The difference between being rational, active, and free and being driven by passion, passive, and unfree is, for Spinoza, a matter of being determined from within or from without. Being determined from within means power, self-realisation,[34] and therefore joy, so Spinoza sets out to show us how this control from within, this shift from passion to reason, can be accomplished.

Ultimately we cannot escape being determined by natural forces outside us, for the force of gravity keeps us on the ground and the need for food makes us hungry; we are liable to illness and will inevitably be killed by disease or the wear and tear of coping with the world. When we are attracted to a woman, afraid of an enemy, or gasping for a drink, we are also in a state of bondage, because though these states may reflect something of our nature, they also represent the pull which an outside object—a lovely woman, a dangerous enemy, or a tasty beverage—exercises on us.

Liberty cannot possibly mean that we forswear women and wine and never flee from danger, still less that we stop eating or avoid illness. Spinoza's point is that we can do from reason what we do from passion. A trivial everyday example can illustrate what I understand him to say. To eat is a necessity, but I only act from passion[35] and am in bondage when I crave food because of its delicious taste. If on the other hand I eat because I have recognised my need for food, my behaviour is determined by reason and therefore from within, and I have entered the realm of freedom. It is not so much that the behaviour has changed (though passion may lead to excess while reason will, by definition, provide correct guidance),[36] as that it becomes differently motivated. This transformation which the acquisition of knowledge itself produces is the great trick by which we pass

from impotence to power and 'blessedness'. This is a striking
anticipation of one of Freud's theories.

Spinoza suggests, in some detail, various procedures for con-
trolling our passions, but it is enough here to summarise the
crux of his theory: the more comprehensive our knowledge and
the more important, extensive, and unchanging its object, the
more fully can this knowledge occupy our minds and so dominate our lives.[37] As it is knowledge of God which fulfils this
requirement most completely and so brings liberation, when we
experience this access of power accompanied by joy we come
to love God as its source.[38] It is, literally, the love of God which
saves us. In Spinoza's mouth this piece of traditional wisdom
becomes much more than a theological platitude or the product
of a mystical revelation, for it emerges—once we grant his definitions—as a demonstrable truth. Put differently, without reference to God, Spinoza's conclusion is that the universe is a
rational order which responds to our reason. If we are entangled
in it without understanding its nature, we are only its passive
victims. The more we understand it, the greater is our role, the
more permanent our influence, the greater our freedom and
happiness.

The Three Kinds of Knowledge

Spinoza combined his conception of reality and picture of man
with a theory of knowledge which is equally relevant for the
development of sociology. It takes for its point of departure the
recognition of the obvious fact that the human body is in constant interaction with its environment. As physical beings we
are sustained, buffeted, and ultimately destroyed by things
around us and constantly receive impressions through our eyes,
ears, nose, tongue, and the surface of our skin.[39] We also im-
pinge both accidentally and deliberately on our environment in
numerous ways. The physical impact of external stimuli triggers
physiological responses: processes in brain, glands, and nerves
which may precipitate some overt behaviour. A pin, let us say,
is pushed into my flesh, nerve cells carry a current to the brain
which, in turn, activates muscles, and I jump. Because, as we
have seen, material events have their counterpart in mental ones,
changes in consciousness run parallel to the physical events I

have referred to.[40] I feel pain, am conscious of something pricking me, and am aware of recoiling or deliberately moving away.

This kind of typical situation (which could equally have been one of seeing or smelling something) provides the basis for three areas of knowledge: knowledge of an external object, of one's body, and of one's mind. Each bit of knowledge is manifestly partial, fragmentary, or, as Spinoza calls it, 'inadequate'.[41] In terms of my illustration, I am aware of something sharp, but it could be a pin or a needle made of steel, silver, or any other metal. What I know of my body from this particular experience is no more adequate. I am aware that the skin on my arm has been punctured but do not know automatically about the complex physiological processes which this has set up. What I know about my mental states is similar: I have become familiar with a sensation of pain and perhaps with some visual or tactile impressions. It certainly does not mean that I have acquired expert knowledge as a psychologist. Experience, possibly augmented by experiments, presents us with a multiplicity of such situations which extend but can never complete our knowledge.

This, then, is Spinoza's description of empirical knowledge. He calls it 'the first kind of knowledge', and in it he includes second-hand knowledge obtained from others when they tell us what they have experienced.[42] All this knowledge is partial, because there is always more to be known about an object and its relations to other objects, and only omniscience could complete the picture. It is also fallible knowledge (or if one prefers, knowledge which may turn out not to be knowledge). This cannot mean that nothing corresponds to our ideas, because that would contradict Spinoza's whole conception that thought and matter are merely two sides of the same reality. It is more that partial knowledge is misleading; something like mislabelling may also occur, whereby an idea is referred to something other than its own physical counterpart.[43]

Spinoza's second kind of knowledge is knowledge of general laws based on what things genuinely have in common (and not on the imprecise generalisations embodied in our classification of objects as 'trees' or 'horses').[44] By identifying these genuinely shared characteristics as quantifiable variables such as extension or weight, Spinoza anticipated the emphasis on what later came to be called primary qualities and marked the development of modern science.

However, the most intriguing, difficult, and seminal aspect of Spinoza's theory of knowledge lies in his conception of a third kind of knowledge, which he calls 'intuitive science'.[45] It is also the part of his philosophy which, though not specially designed for that purpose, has had the most important bearing on the methodology of the social sciences and proved influential in its development. Though this third kind of knowledge plays a crucial role in Spinoza's whole philosophy, it is not discussed very explicitly, and because it is new and original, it needs interpreting. I take it to be knowledge of individual things in their full individuality, which means seeing them within the network of their relationships to other individual things and grasping their place within the hierarchy of systems. It is not a matter of remembering something learned mechanically, arriving at some particular conclusion by inferences from general principles or previous knowledge, but describes—and this is consistent with the normal meaning of 'intuitive'—a form of immediate apprehension which is, however, neither a feeling nor a hunch but genuine knowledge.

One way of making clearer what Spinoza means by this form of knowledge is to suggest that it would be the way in which God knows the world, though, of course, this can only be a metaphorical way of speaking as God, for Spinoza, is not a person and thus can have no knowledge in the ordinary sense of the word. Once we allow ourselves this licence we can readily see that he could not possibly know reality through experience, learning, or inference. Only an imperfect intellect like that of man starts from ignorance and then, gradually, coming across things and learning about their nature, builds up a limited stock of knowledge. God's knowledge must be unmediated and complete awareness of reality in all its details and all its intricacy. Individuals are known to him in their uniqueness and he does not need generalisations.

For us limited human beings such divine knowledge—intuitive science in its fullest sense—can only be an ideal or limiting concept. To have complete knowledge of an individual thing we must see it in its full context, which in the last resort is the structure of the whole universe; such knowledge is obviously beyond us. We can, however, speak meaningfully of intuitive knowledge in a more limited sense as an imperfect approximation to an ideal limit. (This is, after all, how Spinoza uses a number of concepts, such as freedom, which strictly only apply to God but can be attributed to men in a limited sense.) An example of such limited but nevertheless genuine intuitive knowledge would be that of a mathematician looking at a geometrical figure and 'seeing' the relationship between various parts and, possibly, some new demonstration of their nature. One must emphasise that this is an immediate insight and not the product of discursive thought. Yet it is far from irrational, for it is only vouchsafed to intelligent, well-stocked, and well-trained minds and can be spelled out afterwards in chains of reasoning. It describes the sudden feeling that pieces of a puzzle have fallen into place which must have occurred when Newton supposedly hit upon the theory of gravity on seeing an apple fall. Traditional philosophy of science has been at a loss how to account for these hunches or flashes of inspiration, but Spinoza gives them a place of honour in his epistemology by calling them the highest kind of knowledge. This is not, however, confined to placing more than usual emphasis on the intuitive origin of explanations but has, as we shall see a further, more specific significance for sociology.

The Scientific Study of Man

Spinoza's thought bears on sociology in different ways, some quite specific, others more general. Before turning to such specific contributions as his views on particular methods or his suggestions of particular hypotheses about the nature of society and man's place in it, I must refer to the most general level on which he influenced the subject. His philosophy of science spelled out most rigorously in rationalist terms and provided a powerful framework and justification for not only the physical sciences, which were rapidly developing in his time, but also the social sciences, which were to emerge a little later.

His identification of God and nature, his psychophysical parallelism, and his insistence on a universal causal order all supported the idea of a world which we could come to know fully by applying rational, scientific methods consistently. For Spinoza the belief that reality was rationally knowable also meant that a unified scientific approach was possible, and this—as students of sociology know—is an issue which continues to divide practitioners of their subject. At one extreme, positivists have stressed the importance of establishing or maintaining universal methods, which for them means assimilating sociological work to the successful practice of the physical sciences.[46] At the other extreme, sociologists (sometimes lumped together under such labels as 'phenomenological sociologists' or 'understanding sociologists') have rejected the idea that their research can resemble that of the sciences, because people are significantly different from other objects or even other animals.[47] Spinoza can be seen as siding with the positivists, and he provides a salutory warning against those antipositivists who have abandoned rigorous testing of theories in favour of impressionistic accounts, chatty anecdotes, and hunches.

On the other hand one must appreciate the thrust of Spinoza's argument in favour of the unity of science in terms of the problems of his own age. In seventeenth-century Europe various factors, the predominant religious traditions foremost among them, conspired to discourage objective research of the human world. People still believed in the devil and witches. The religious view of life was still strong and presented an obstacle to the objective study of man, by posing such questions as Can a scientific psychology do justice to an immortal soul tainted by sin yet containing the image of God? Can social science properly appreciate marriage, which is a sacrament? Can political science penetrate the mystery of divine kingship? How can history explain events which are the products of God's inscrutable will? or How can any social science explain mental illness or crime if they might be the work of the devil? Descartes had done a great deal to destroy superstitions and prejudices which hindered the development of free science, but his dualism was also designed to protect the soul from a crudely scientific analysis. It is in this context that Spinoza's massive arguments in favour of a single, law-governed, and therefore knowable reality and his insistence that there could be no conflict between science and religion were so important. Today this particular battle has been largely won, and few people will give religious grounds for treating the human world as a mystery beyond the reach of science. Nevertheless, the feeling that a cold, scientific approach is somewhat offensive and inappropriate when applied to man lingers on, and some investigators, recoiling from behaviouristic approaches modelled on the physical sciences, have considered rigour in their methods almost improper, or at least have taken the question of how truth can be established too lightly. Being scientific, in the sense of being rigorous in one's methods and as objective as possible in one's approach, remains important and is more fundamental than the question of how far the methods of different disciplines must vary.

Within the context of Spinoza's overall advocacy of a scientific approach, his insistence on causal explanations and rejection of teleological ones[48] is specially significant and has a direct bearing on contemporary debates within sociology. Spinoza rejected explanation in terms of purposes for several reasons, of which one was that it appeared to invert the temporal order by explaining an event of the present in terms of a pull exercised by something in the future. Another was that reality, being perfect, could not strive for anything, could not have a purpose. But the reason of the greatest methodological importance is that the search for purposes is ultimately futile. To explain any purpose we have identified, we must relate it to a higher, more comprehensive purpose that it subserves. Thus, ascending through a hierarchy of purposes, we arrive at the question What is the purpose of reality as a whole, the purpose of God? Even if, contrary to Spinoza's view, God had a purpose, we could not know it. So we arrive at the idea of a mysterious universe or the inscrutable will of God, and what was intended as an explanation becomes a tool of obscurantism.

Spinoza does not, of course, go to the absurd length of avoiding all talk of purposes. He recognises that human behaviour can be purposive whether people act individually or jointly pursue a common purpose. However, the question pressed so sharply in Spinoza's philosophy—How far can purposes serve as explanations?—is highly pertinent for sociology. Social changes, the development of institutions, and booms and slumps are, notoriously, not the realisations of anyone's purposes. In some cases it is impossible to identify individuals or groups who aimed at the actual result; in others the result even runs counter to anyone's aims. It is, then, all too easy to introduce the notions of a 'hidden hand' or 'the cunning of reason'[49] or even to suspect some plotting minority secretly at work. No harder and even more dangerous is to leaave the source of purposes undefined or to define it as a strange monster like the national will or the state. Earlier we saw Plato's metaphysical solution to this problem. Spinoza's warning of the danger of loosely using purposes as explanations remains a timely warning.

However, his most important contribution to the future of sociology is his theoretical justifications of the systematic study of individual entities, which is contained in his discussion of intuitive science. The undoubted fact that sociology deals very largely with individual entities rather than with whole classes of objects has been frequently ignored, minimised, or even denied. Its subject matter is usually a particular group, association, institution, or society. It may be as specific as family relations in a particular village or industrial conflict in a particular factory, or as comprehensive as the trend towards rationalisation in modern industrial society; but these are unique, individual entities and not family life or society in general. This state of affairs has been a source of embarrassment to sociologists, because they have found themselves unable to produce the high-level generalisations and universal laws which are the aim of science and have hoped for a Newton of the social sciences who would remedy the situation. Many sociologists try to imitate the methods of the social sciences so as to bring nearer the blessed day when sociology too can discover general laws.

No doubt something can be—and indeed has been—said about how societies in general function or what all family life has in common, but it appears by and large trivial in comparison with the rich detail we like to acquire about particular societies, detail which sociology has, in fact, provided. The attraction of Spinoza's philosophy, not least for the sociologist, is that he provided a rational underpinning for a form of rigorous study which does not aim at establishing general laws. The alternative of explaining a thing in terms of the specific context to which it belongs (the whole of which it is a part) and its own structure (the parts it consists of) is familiar to common sense and obviously used by the sciences. In sociology this mode of thought acquires a particularly important role which makes Spinoza's attempt to show that it is a respectable and rational cognitive approach in its own right so liberating to sociologists.

It is obviously not enough to accept that some things are structured and can be explained both in terms of their own structure and the larger structure they belong to. But if we can assume that this structuring is pervasive, it is possible for sociology to be a systematic discipline aiming at a comprehensive knowledge of social life, rather than a patchwork of information. Spinoza, as we have seen, makes this assumption about reality at large. For him the universe is not like a box full of odds and ends, but more like an organism which functions as a whole but contains parts which in turn function as wholes. Sociologists need not stop to decide if this is a plausible overall picture to find it a persuasive hypothesis about social life. It *is* fruitful to assume that the way individual schools are run is affected by and will in turn affect the educational system of a country, and that the latter has its role to play in the economic and social life of the country.

Spinoza's intuitive science, which comprehends individual entities in their full individuality by seeing them in their contexts, is the cognitive approach most adjusted to a universe which is systematically structured as an individual consisting of individuals. By calling this intuitive comprehension the highest kind of knowledge, and thus challenging the dominance of the search for general laws, Spinoza gave enormous encouragement to such disciplines as biology and philology, which are more concerned with structure than with uniformities. Eventually his theories provided intellectual backbone to a particular method which has a long tradition but has emerged from relative obscurity into the limelight only during the last hundred years: hermeneutics,[50] which clearly shares with Spinoza's approach a preoccupation with the individual and the technique of disentangling parts within a whole. His contribution to this development alone would give him a significant place in the prehistory of sociology.

To these very general methodological issues concerning the unity of science, causal explanation, and the study of individuals we can add a number of more specific points on which Spinoza also exercised an influence on sociology. One of these, probably the most important single point in his exposition of human nature and its dependence on social contexts, is his rationalist insistence that reason is itself the essential feature of individual and social life and not just a tool for other desirable ends. His view of society as the necessary basis for the rational life and for the acquisition and spread of knowledge provides a distinctive and interesting angle of approach for the social scientist. Certainly such features of modern life as mass production, bureaucracy, economic planning, and international organisations have been treated by sociologists as attempts to achieve rational order, explanations which are none the worse for applying a model of rationality rather than providing a realistic description.[51]

Another theory of Spinoza's which has special significance for sociology is his view that mind and matter are alternative ways of looking at reality, because he draws from it the methodological conclusion that explanations, if they are to be intelligible, must remain within one sphere or the other. Mental events must be explained in terms of other mental events, physical ones in terms of physical events. It makes sense to suggest that coffee stimulates the brain, because we can envisage how such an effect may be produced and so test whether it is true or false. Again, it makes sense to suggest that Max Weber's use of *Verstehen* was influenced by Wilhelm Dilthey's philosophy, because here too it is possible to understand how one thought or theory can give rise to another. To suggest, however, that Weber framed his theory of *Verstehen* because he ate a lot of beef would, on Spinoza's principle, be both nonsensical and sterile. Because the illustration I have chosen is both simple and implausible it may seem very obvious that Spinoza is right, that it is superfluous and trivial to stress it. However, the history of the social sciences has produced a host of theories which are of the same kind but have escaped criticism because the obscurity of the connection between physical and mental factors is hidden by the complexity and portentousness of the theory. It has been argued that climate and other geographical conditions, or racial characteristics, influence cultural products and even scientific theories. Even more famous is the Marxist theory about the relation between superstructure and infrastructure (that is, between mental creations and physical conditions). There is nothing wrong with establishing correlations between phenomena of different types (and nothing in Spinoza to suggest that there is), nor is there anything to be said against theorising about such correlations if we can make it meaningful. Spinoza's principle is not a dogma to be accepted blindly. The problem is to make these correlations meaningful, to produce coherent accounts of the mechanisms through which alleged causal connections work. That is, it is only meaningful to say that the social structure of a country affects its dominant philosophy, or that the distribution of the means of production makes a difference to the educational system, if we can be clear *how* these affects are produced. If Spinoza is right—and he certainly has a case—we must be careful to translate social structure or the distribution of the means of production into human thoughts and theories before their connection to other thoughts and theories can become clear.

The relevance of Spinoza's nominalism for sociology has been referred to earlier. Nominalism means rejecting the idea that general terms necessarily represent a class of objects with significant common characteristics, an attitude which is more than justified in the case of socially defined concepts. Even if Spinoza were wrong about our descriptions of nature, he has a point about the way we talk about people and institutions, because there our laziness or prejudices tend to produce distorting stereotypes.

Finally it is worth recalling the usefulness of Spinoza's definition of individuals, because it has a bearing on methodological issues still under discussion today. One issue concerns the kind of entities which sociology can treat as real and use in its explanations. Social thinkers have attributed to entities we habitually talk about, such as families, societies, or nations, an awesome reality and the status of superpersons by talking about 'national will', a 'folk soul', and 'collective consciousness', but it has also been maintained that only individual human beings are real entities which think and have a will, while nations, societies, and similar corporate entities are only artificial constructions consisting of individual human beings and their relations to each other.[52] Both these positions have absurd

methodological consequences. Taking the idea of collective entities with a soul or will of their own too seriously leads to un-
testable theories and so to mystery-mongering, because it
becomes impossible to provide objective criteria about what the
'national soul' craves. To insist instead, as methodological individualism does, that discussions of social phenomena all be
translated into talk about the motives and actions of individual
people is equally misguided and impracticable. Such an ordinary, and perfectly understandable, statement as 'Britain declared war on Germany' does not mean that the British Foreign
Secretary declared war on the German Ambassador (or the members of the British Cabinet on the Kaiser). It is more than doubtful
that even combining any number of such statements about individuals could produce an equivalent to the original statement;
but even if it did, it would then be patently impossible to test
a theory about numerous individuals of which some remain
anonymous.

Spinoza's definition of what is to be treated as an individual
provides a perfectly lucid and practical solution to the problem.
Individuals exist and can be identified insofar as they produce
unitary results. Human beings fire rifles but states wage war.
We remain firmly on the ground of experience as long as we do
not attribute additional, hidden qualities to the individuals we
use in our theories, and this approach eliminates a host of
pseudoproblems.

Spinoza's highly speculative system is at first glance not the
most obvious choice for sociologists to make for their reading.
Yet it contains, as I hope to have shown, a wealth of ideas which
they will find thought-provoking.

5 . *Kant*: The Critique of Reason

Kant gave the philosophy of reason a decisive new turn by directing critical attention to the powers of reason itself. With more subtlety and penetration than anyone before or after him, he analysed the mind's capacity to know and to direct human actions. These investigations transformed the intellectual landscape of Europe, leaving their indelible imprint on all subsequent philosophy and inspiring theologians, political thinkers, and poets. (Wordsworth and Coleridge are outstanding examples of English writers profoundly affected by Kantian philosophy.)

His contemporaries thought the explosive force of Kant's ideas almost demonic. Theologians called him 'the all-shattering Kant', and Coleridge likened his influence to being 'gripped by a giant's hand'. Yet nothing could be more reassuringly pedestrian than his quiet personality and his almost ludicrously well-ordered life. The son of a saddler, reputedly of Scottish descent, he spent all his life in East Prussia. Indeed, apart from a period as a tutor on a Prussian estate, he never set foot outside Koenigsberg, where he studied and became a lecturer and eventually a professor. Like Plato, Descartes, and Spinoza he remained unmarried and regulated his days with a painstaking, indeed pedantic, precision. He lectured in the early morning, spent a longish period with friends over a midday meal (the only one he ate), went for an hour's walk in the afternoon, and slept for eight hours at night. All the rest of the time, year in, year out, he singlemindedly devoted to his thinking and writing.

Kant shared with the other philosophers discussed in this book a common concern with reason and other important attitudes, such as the belief that he was revolutionising philosophy by placing it on more secure foundations. He also shared with them a width of interest ranging over philosophy, the sciences, and the practical affairs of men. Not only was he a trained mathematician, but he lectured on military engineering and was the author (with Laplace) of a cosmological theory. He also had an absorbing interest in almost anything which concerned humanity. He wrote thoughtfully about history, politics, legislation, government, revolution, international cooperation, education, and the penal system. In his later years he lectured entertainingly on anthropology, discussing among other topics such questions as the mental differences between men and women or the reason why people smoked. Paranormal phenomena (of which he was sceptical) and artistic questions also attracted his attention. All these subjects he approached in a lively manner and was, by all accounts, a popular lecturer and entertaining conversationalist. Though he spent most of his life in his house in Koenigsberg, it was far from an ivory tower.

Yet Kant differed from the other philosophers in some respects as strikingly as he resembled them in others, because the new intellectual climate of his time (1724–1804) affected his outlook and the philosophical role he played. Plato was present at the very beginning of rational and scientific inquiry in Europe, and Descartes participated with Spinoza in the creation of modern science; Kant could already look back on a majestic intellectual achievement culminating in the work of Newton. His role was to consolidate, assess, and justify existing accomplishments, rather than pioneer new ones.

Kant's outlook was also affected by social and political conditions which were very different from those faced by the earlier thinkers. Plato had witnessed a society in which faiths and old traditions were breaking up, Descartes and Spinoza a world of religious wars; Kant saw considerable progress in the triumph of reason, for even such violent upheavals as the American and French revolutions were conducted in its name. He was thus able to advocate reason more sedately and with more critical detachment than his predecessors.

What also distinguishes Kant from the others is that he wrote, at least in his main works, as an academic. Plato, though also a teacher in his own academy, wrote his dialogues for a wider public. Descartes and Spinoza, like most other major philosophers of the seventeenth and eighteenth centuries, such as Hobbes, Bacon, Leibniz, Hume, Voltaire, and Rousseau, held no public teaching appointments. Descartes wrote for the educated layman; Spinoza, one feels, for himself and eternity. Kant was a state-employed professional teacher of philosophy, the first great modern philosopher to be a professor, and we note a corresponding change in style and approach. Though he showed that he could write elegantly in some of his minor essays and also occasionally achieved majestic eloquence in his main works, he usually wrote rather cumbersomely; his arguments are repetitive, highly technical, and sometimes pedantic. Because subsequent philosophers, also professors, felt impelled to imitate him in order to appear as philosophically respectable, one can say that Kant taught philosophers to write badly. It is, however, a testimony to his greatness that through the husk of his tiresome verbiage there shine the most dazzlingly exciting arguments in the history of philosophy.

Knowledge as the Mind's Creation

As with the other philosophers, we must first get an overall picture of Kant's philosophy before we can appreciate his contribution to sociology. If we are to gain an idea of the revolution he wrought in philosophy, we need to understand the problem he confronted. Brought up on the rationalism of Leibniz and Christian A. Wolff, who like Spinoza believed that reality was knowable because it was rationally structured, he was nevertheless one of the first to recognise the far-reaching and destructive implications of Hume's sceptical arguments. From the traditional tenet of empiricism—that all knowledge derives from experience—Hume had deduced that we could not know the very things which formed the cornerstones of rationalist systems (a permanent self, substance, and causality), because what we experience are states of mind, not a self; qualities of things, not substance; and sequences of events, not a link between them. Even more alarmingly, philosophy itself became impossible, for clearly Hume's own philosophic conclusions were not based on experience and thus, on his own principle, could make no claim to represent knowledge.

Kant was profoundly shocked by Hume's arguments, for although he accepted that the attack on rationalist metaphysics was conclusive, he could not concede that our knowledge of a substantial, causally ordered world was illusory. We experience and know, he was convinced, much more than the stream of impressions which empiricism allows for. In fact he turned the tables on the empiricists in a devastating attack on their concept of experience by accusing—justifiably I think—empiricists like Hume of assuming that we experience such things as rolling billiard balls while defining experience solely in terms of sense data. A billiard ball is, however, not a coloured patch (or succession of such patches) plus a clicking noise, but a solid object persisting in time.

Paradoxically enough, Kant, who is a philosopher's philosopher in his technical language and subtle arguments, took the side of robust common sense against philosophers like Hume or, for that matter, Descartes, who made themselves ridiculous, he thought, by asking such farfetched questions as Do we really know that there is an external world? Can we be sure that we are not dreaming? or Is knowledge possible at all? Without being shaken by the philosophers' doubts or needing their assurance, we are convinced that we can see ships sailing by or rain falling, and can even draw scientific conclusions from our observations. If doubt creeps in, we allay it by looking again, repeating our experiments, or checking our calculations. So for Kant (as for Spinoza, but in a more modest, nonmetaphysical way) knowledge was a fact. The philosopher's job was to explain *how* such knowledge was possible or, in other words, what is involved in and presupposed by our capacity for acquiring knowledge.

Even at this early stage it may be worth mentioning how relevant this way of defining the philosopher's job is for sociology. Scepticism about everyday observations or the theories of physics are, if not due to mental derangement, manifestly a philosophic contrivance, but doubts about knowledge of the human world, spawned by philosophic theories, have been taken quite seriously even by social scientists themselves.

However, what kind of foundations of knowledge could Kant be looking for once he had rejected the empiricist explanation as inadequate and the rationalist one as ill-supported? His answer is that the powers of the mind themselves provide the unchanging structures on which we can rely. The mind, by which he means the capacities, faculties, or mental equipment which we all share and which functions in all of us in the same way, is active in organising and structuring the impressions it receives and thereby imposes its own patterns on experience. He called this view his Copernican Revolution because he thought he could explain the basic features of the observed world in terms of the knowing subject's activities, much as Copernicus had explained the apparent movements of the heavenly bodies in terms of the observer's movement with the earth.[1]

This assumption accounts for the knowledge we have as the conception of a passive mind cannot. If the mind were just a mirror on which reality is reflected, or a slate on which experience writes its letters, there could be no reason, other than the speculative claims of rationalism, why we should be confident that our impressions represent abiding features of reality, that the future will resemble the present, or one part of the universe the rest. Just as a photograph cannot assure me that a person always does and will look like the image in the picture, so the experience that fire burns wood today cannot, from the empiricist's point of view, guarantee that it will at other times. But if the regularities we attribute to the world of experience are imposed by the mind acting according to rules of its own, then we can rely on the knowledge we gain about them. If, to illustrate this point, we were forced to wear irremovable green spectacles, all the world would be tinged green. Though we might not know what we would encounter next, we would confidently predict that it would be green. (What these structures of the mind are, we shall consider presently, but they are not, as this metaphor may seem to suggest, colours.)

The world which the mind structures cannot be ultimate reality, because we are not omnipotent; but the world as it presents itself in our experience, the real world of trees, houses and people is 'phenomenal' but not a fantasy world.[2] It is subject to the principles of cognition, because it can only be reality as it appears to the mind. It is meaningless to ask what reality is like in itself or as seen by an intelligence different from ours, because we can only see and think it as we do. Whatever ultimately impinges on the mind must be thought of as an X, because we only know it when and as it is absorbed by our cognitive apparatus. The mind in knowing something can be likened more to a spider gobbling up a fly than a tablet receiving an imprint, as long as we conceive fly and spider to be only observable while the one devours the other.

Thus all knowledge is, in Kant's phrase, 'transcendentally subjective', that is, seen from the point of view of a subject. Its subjectivity does not, however, prevent knowledge from being 'empirically objective', because your mind and mine organise their impressions basically in the same way, so that when you see a table, so do I. The subjective differences due to different perspectives, colour blindness, or prejudices are something else again.

The Transcendental Deduction

Two characteristic features of Kant's approach may be worth mentioning before we turn to his account of *how* the mind structures its experience. One of them is that Kant's case is largely based on, and indeed is at its strongest when it deals with, ordinary, even trivial cases of knowledge, like seeing a house or knowing that two plus two is four. One might think that the analysis of more complex and controversial examples of knowledge, say Heisenberg's Uncertainty Principle, Russell and Whitehead's *Principia Mathematica*, or Parsons's Functionalism, might be more rewarding, but this is not so. In these more complex cases, though philosophy has something to say about them, problems requiring special expertise overlay the fundamental issues which are the philosopher's real concern. His problem is not so much to illuminate the unknown and difficult, but to make us aware of what is involved in what seems so simple that we take it for granted.

The other characteristic of Kant's whole approach is a type of argument which he designed for his purpose and which recurs throughout his *Critique of Pure Reason*: the transcendental deduction.[3] Once we understand the structure of this type of argument, we can appreciate how Kant's philosophical approach differed from a psychological or sociological one. This will protect us from midunderstanding Kant's theories about the mind. They are not psychological or sociological hypotheses, and his influence on sociology was not that of an amateur sociologist.

Kant's transcendental deduction takes the form of concluding that something exists because it is the necessary condition of something else which actualy exists. (To put it in logical form: If, and only if A then B. B. Therefore A. Without the 'only if' the deduction is, of course, just a howler. It does not follow from If it rains the pavement is wet; the pavement is wet, that it has rained, for the road may have been sprinkled.) The validity of this kind of argument thus depends on the possibility of establishing that there is a necessary and irreplaceable condition for the occurrence of something we know to exist. To establish the negative, that there could be no other possible cause of something, is notoriously difficult; but readers will be able to judge for themselves how convincing Kant's case is.

A deduction of the form just described is, in Kant's terminology, 'transcendental' if what is inferred lies outside, or transcends, what is empirically given. For Kant's purpose it is essential that such arguments should be possible, because unless we can come to know the conditions of experience on grounds independent from experience, we are moving in a vicious circle, trying to explain experience by experience. This would be as illuminating as the following exchange: How is it possible for us to see? Because we have eyes. How do we know we have eyes? Because we can see them. But how is it possible to see them? And so on ad infinitum, as in the song about the hole in the bucket.

This point has a crucial bearing on the sociology of knowledge, to which we shall turn later, and a single illustration of a circular argument typical of the kind which Kant was concerned to avoid will prepare us for that topic. From many possible examples let us choose a quotation from Max Horkheimer's *Critical Theory*: 'Reason cannot become transparent to itself as long as men act as members of an organism which lacks reason.'[4] If this statement is supposed to mean more than the platitude that perfection eludes human beings, it must suggest that we cannot rely on our reason and, therefore, on our knowledge in a less than rational society. But then how could we reliably know that we live in an irrational society, let alone have an idea of how to remedy it? The circle involved condemns the statement to futility, for if we know that our society lacks reason and know what that means, our reason has become 'transparent to itself' and therefore does not require membership in a rational organisation. (There would be no circle, of course, if Horkheimer were referring to organisations less fortunate than the perfectly rational one of which he himself was a member, but I do not think that he means that.) A larger issue, the autonomy of reason, is involved here, and to this I shall return in the next chapter.

Kant was determined to avoid the kind of circular argument to which Horkheimer succumbed, and that is why he insisted on using transcendental deductions, that is, rational arguments about the basis of experience which owed nothing to experience. It is irrelevant to him whether the objects or processes which he postulates as necessary conditions of our experience are accessible to experience or not. He insists, for example, that we are not directly aware of the intellectual processes which (according to him) must take place if our sensations are to be translated into an awareness of objects. He frequently, and quite happily, suggests that *how* an essential mental process occurred is a mystery or 'secret buried in the depth of the soul'.[5]

Though our knowledge of the existence of these mental processes cannot be derived from experience, there is no compelling reason why they should not also be accessible to experience. Philosophy need not put up 'no trespassing' signs around any parts of the universe. Though philosophic theories cannot be based directly on sociological evidence, do not depend for confirmation on it, and cannot be refuted by it, there is no reason why sociology should not cover the same ground and even confirm, or converge with, philosophic theories. Indeed there is every reason for such convergence. That is why philosophic theories can inspire sociological hypotheses.

The Factors Involved in Experience

By focusing attention on fundamental cases of knowledge and applying to them his transcendental deductions, Kant tried to establish the factors presupposed in cognition. In following the line of his argument we note first among the necessary features of the knowing mind our capacity to receive a variety of sense data, such as sounds or sights.[6] These data are given to the mind from outside, and without them, Kant concedes to empiricism, no knowledge would be possible. In receiving them the mind is passive. The second characteristic of human cognition is that impressions are received in a temporal order, and some of them, such as visual and tactual ones, in a spatial order as well.[7] Kant emphasised that time and space are not objects (that is, space is not a kind of box) or characteristics of ultimate reality, but necessary forms which our experience takes. That is why we can have formal knowledge, not derived from experience, about temporal and spatial relationships. (Geometry, the nonempirical science of formal spatial relationships, is an example.)

The third feature of the mind is its capacity for synthesis, for putting together the manifold of impressions it receives. This capacity, which constitutes the active part of the mind, is necessary because—and this assumption is a cornerstone of Kant's entire approach—we only experience connections, patterns, and composite wholes if the mind has done the connecting and putting together.[8]

From this assumption he deduced a further feature of the knowing mind, its transcendental unity; for if things need connecting, they must be connected by and in a single mind.[9] The question whether I have or have not some kind of inner experience which convinces me that I am the same person as I was a few moments before is irrelevant, because that would be merely an empirical argument, while what matters is a transcendental deduction. In fact, a summary of Kant's argument on this matter gives an excellent illustration of such a deduction. We are confident that we can see a house or hear a melody, and to deny it would drive scepticism to an absurd length. But unless the consciousness which is aware of the first note is the *same* as that which hears the second, no one person could claim that he had heard the melody. If the observer of the roof is not identical with the one who looks at the ground floor, neither has seen the house. This unity of consciousness is therefore, whether we observe it or not, established as a necessary condition of a feat we know we can accomplish.

We must, however, clearly distinguish this transcendentally deduced knowing 'I' which collates all the messages received from the senses, from the empirical self. Here Kant spells out an argument already adumbrated by Descartes. When I speak of myself as a person with particular physical features, a history of my own, a name, and a job, I am referring to myself as an object of knowledge while presupposing the process by which all this is known. The knowing 'I' is as little part of the empirical knowledge which it achieves as the lens is of the photograph it takes. Of course we can fix our attention on the knowing subject, just as we can take a separate photograph of the lens; but then the knowing subject has become another object, and there is a new cognitive 'I' which has receded a further step. Thus what we know of the knowing subject *as* knowing subject is necessarily the product of a transcendental deduction and never of observation.

The next stage of the argument takes us to the organising principles by which the mind structures the material given it by the senses. Sense impressions located in space and time and apprehended by a unitary consciousness still do not add up to the kind of world we are familiar with, but present merely a dreamlike flow or, in Kant's own words, a 'rhapsody of perceptions'.[10] But in fact we perceive persisting objects as being related to each other according to causal laws. When, for example, I see a table I am attributing the hardness I feel and the shape I see to a persistent object which, I am confident, is there because it had been placed there and will remain there unless removed or destroyed. If it flickered in and out of existence, I would not think that I was seeing a table. All this is not an optional way of seeing things; I have no choice about continuing to see the same object, or a sequence of events in a particular order. My sensations have been ordered and assembled in a way which subjects my experience to a firm constraint. What constrains us, according to Kant, are the necessary rules which the mind imposes on its operations.[11]

What specifically distinguishes seeing a house from a chaos of impressions is the concept we superimpose on our impressions and thereby organise them. In other words the concept provides a rule as to what is involved if something is to be called a house. Data which are not conceptualised in this way are in Kant's words 'blind'; concepts which do not refer to such data are 'empty'.[12] This is one of the often quoted formulations in which Kant presents his compromise between empiricism and rationalism. The empiricists were right in insisting that sense data are indispensible for knowledge but wrong in assuming that these data can, by themselves and without aid from intellectual operations, constitute knowledge. The rationalists were right in stressing the necessary role of thought but wrong in concluding that it could produce anything substantial without being related to sense impressions.

Concepts like 'house' are empirical; they have been coined in response to specific experiences which also provide a test for the appropriate use of the term. These empirical concepts, as sociologists know and have cause to discuss, are socially determined because they reflect special, socially conditioned experiences and are expressed in a language which is itself a social product. Some societies have no houses and therefore no concept for them; others may have such divergent types of houses that they find it convenient to coin separate concepts for each type.

Kant's point is that over and above the empirical concepts the mind also uses a number of transcendental concepts which are formal and very general organising principles.[13] Because they represent necessary conditions of knowledge, transcendental concepts are universal and therefore not socially conditioned. Indeed they provide the underpinning for socially conditioned concepts. Kant called these fundamental, nonempirical concepts 'categories' and attempted their transcendental deduction.

Kant thought that he could demonstrate that there is a fixed number, namely twelve, of these categories, but that is one of the more doubtful parts of his theory. Not all the categories are equally important, and the most significant ones are causality and substance, which play a crucial role in our everyday judgments. Both causality and substance have provided focal points of controversy between rationalists and empiricists. For the sake of simplicity I shall confine my illustrations to the case of causality.

As a category, causality can be spelled out in the statement Everything has a cause, or formulated as the rule Whenever you want to understand an object or event you can and must look for its cause. How did we derive this concept, and what authority has its formulation as a statement or rule? Particular causal judgements are clearly based on experience. Without experience we would not know that fire burns wood or that rain wets the pavement. But the general categorial judgement is not so derived. We do not, and cannot, inspect 'everything' so as to conclude that everything has a cause. Far from deriving causality from experience, we presuppose it when we approach experience. If my lighter fails to work I examine it on the assumption that one or another thing, perhaps lack of petrol or a worn-out flint, is the cause. If someone were to suggest that I am wasting my time because there may be *no* cause, I would think this not merely unlikely but absurd and even alarming. All this suggests that we bring the concept of causality to bear on our experience as a means of organising our impressions.

For Kant it was not enough to note that we in fact presuppose causality and the other categories when we look at the world. To provide a transcendental deduction of the categories he had to show that without them we could not have the experiences we actually have.[14] All our impressions, Kant noted at the start of his argument, follow each other in irreversible succession. Within a very small range we may take in several impressions simultaneously, but largely they come one after the other. If (to use Kant's own illustrations) we let our eyes wander over a house, we see one part of it after the other; when we see a ship sail past, we see first its bow and later its stern. Yet we have no difficulty about distinguishing between looking at an object and observing an event, for in the latter case the sequence of impressions is imposed on me while in the former I can observe simultaneously existing parts in what order I like. Indeed, not only can we distinguish the sequence of impressions in the mind from a sequence in the world outside us, but we can even appreciate that the one may be the reverse of the other. We may first note that the room is warm and only afterwards that the stove is lit, but we have no difficulty in realising that lighting the stove preceded and is the cause of the warmth.

The reader may think that the distinction between the order in which events occur in the world and the sequence of our impressions is obvious and unproblematic. He must remember, however, that for Kant the outside world, as much as our inner experience, consists of impressions and is an appearance governed by the ordering activity of the mind. Thus the question arises how we can distinguish the order in which the mind perceives something from an order which it *attributes* to the world. Kant's answer is that in seeing objects the mind finds itself constrained by rules which, though of its own making, rigidly govern the way we perceive the relations between impressions. The objective world we live in is not just given, but is constituted by this process. If this conclusion remains difficult for common sense to swallow, one must recall that it is the direct consequence of Kant's Copernican Revolution. Because it is a revolution it requires adjusting to. If knowledge is to be explained in terms of an active mind imposing its order on the world of experience, then the distinction between an incoherent reverie and the perception of a 'real' event cannot be made in terms of the one being internally, the other externally, conditioned. Instead we must distinguish between what is and what is not construed by the rules in the mind which constitute an objective world.

Reason as the Source of Morality

Kant's moral philosophy is as original and important as his epistemology and equally relevant for sociology. This philosophy was developed in a number of major works of which the *Critique of Practical Reason* is the most substantial, but the *Groundwork of the Metaphysic of Morals* the most striking. Most of my references are to the latter work because it contains, in concise form, the most characteristic and original features of Kant's moral philosophy. At the centre of this philosophy is the idea that reason is practical, which for Kant meant capable of moving men to action by its own principles. He arrived at this idea by tackling two related questions: What is the meaning and role of morality? What can be the source of moral principles?

Kant's moral philosophy accepts that we make moral judgements, just as his epistemology accepts that we possess knowledge. He therefore does not consider it his job either to prove that there is morality or to tell people how to become moral. (The latter would be quite absurd, he thinks, because not having read Kant could never be a valid excuse for not knowing what you should do.)[15] Instead his questions here are the equivalent of those he poses in his search for the presuppositions involved in knowledge.

To discover the meaning of moral judgements Kant examines what distinguishes them from other judgements. They are not about wishes, for though we may wish someone well or ill, if we do nothing about it, that is morally neutral even if it indicates a nice or nasty disposition. Nor are moral judgements about individual human characteristics, for a self-controlled murderer is not morally superior to a self-indulgent one.[16] Nor are they about intentions, because we can morally distinguish between two acts which are both intended to please a person by giving him a present, one unselfishly, the other 'from an ulterior motive'.[17] Moral judgement does not depend on the consequences of an action, either.[18] The judgment surely comes down on the side of the man who does his best but through ignorance or ill luck achieves undesirable results, and against a man of ill-will who by accident achieves nothing or even something desirable.

Particularly striking for students of sociology may be Kant's point that morality has nothing directly to do with social utility and the preservation of an orderly society. His argument can be summarised as follows. Any social aim which can be accomplished through moral control can be achieved by other means. We can, let us say, reduce death on the roads by motorists' becoming more conscientious, but also by their becoming more afraid of heavy penalities. If, then, there is something worthwhile in motorists' acting from conscience rather than fear, it cannot be due to its social utility.

It should be clear by now from the catalogue of what moral judgements are not that they are directed towards our motives and nothing else.[19] But what can the right motive, which Kant calls 'good will' be? We have already eliminated social utility and prudence. We can add feeling to the list, because according to Kant there is no moral virtue in doing something because you enjoy doing it or because you like someone.[20] Kant concludes that acting for the sake of morality itself, that is, doing something because it is right, alone constitutes the purity of motive on which morality depends.[21] The only source of such a pure motive—as Kant also tries to show by a separate line of argument—can be reason itself. We must pursue this second argument before we can conclude our answer to the question about the meaning and role of morality.

Moral judgements are invariably universal and categorical. The statements Maybe lying is wrong, and For some people lying is wrong, are not acceptable as moral judgements because they are not universal and categorical.[22] These characteristics essential for moral judgements make it impossible that they should derive from experience, which yields only probable conclusions; nor can they be an expression of feeling or taste, because if they were like preferring wine to beer or being attracted to outdoor sports, they could not be universalised. They cannot be derived from examples (like that of Jesus), either, because the moral perfection of the example would have to be established independently; nor can they derive from the command of God, because unless we have already judged God to be morally perfect, subjection to his power could not be moral.[23]

Reason, by contrast, qualifies as a source of moral judgements because it can yield universal and certain judgments in morality as it does, for example, in mathematics. Reason is also, as Kant had already demonstrated to his satisfaction in the *Critique of Pure Reason*, the spontaneous source of universally valid rules or principles. We may therefore conclude that practical reason produces the rules for moral action just as theoretical reason lays down the rules for organising our experience.

Man's rationality consists in the power to make and follow rules or, as Kant put it, to 'act in accordance with the idea of a law, while everything in the universe merely acts according to law'.[24] Man at his most rational when these rules spring purely from his reason. The moral law fulfils this condition, because unlike such rules as those of the highway code, it owes nothing to the world of experience. But what can the content of such a law possibly be? What can reason command when we have excluded all reference to experience and shown that neither intentions nor consequences matter? Kant answers consistency, conformity to universal rules, in other words lawfulness itself.[25] Kant's own formulation—one of many versions of what he called the 'categorical imperative'—runs, 'Act only on that maxim whereby thou canst at the same time will that it should become a universal law'.[26] This is the purely formal expression of the demand of reason for universality and impartiality, a characteristic also apparent in such biblical injunctions as 'Do unto others as you would have them do unto you' and 'love thy neighbour as thyself' or such homely sayings as 'What is sauce for the goose is sauce for the gander.' None of these formulations tells us specifically what we should do or how we should love our neighbour. Reason simply demands that we should act consistently on the same principle and so not make an exception of ourselves or claim special privileges. This, Kant claimed, was the perennial core of morality.

Kant himself gives many illustrations of how this formal principle pinpoints what is the essence of morality or immorality and can serve as a criterion of whether we have chosen morally or not. Could it be right to steal? You try to universalise the right to steal and find that the point of stealing is to keep what you have stolen; surely you do not want to universalise everybody's right to take it from you again. Stealing only makes sense if you want to make an exception of yourself.[27]

For a purely rational being, reason would be the automatic law of his being, his will a holy will.[28] But man is a creature also governed by impulses and desires, and is thus for Kant a dual creature, partly an animal belonging to the phenomenal world perceived by our senses, partly a rational being belonging to the realm of reason. This duality is a cause of conflict, because man's two sides are likely to pull in different directions. Following the voice of reason (and so of morality) may be genuinely against our interests as material beings and involve sacrifices. This is why the voice of reason is perceived by man as duty (usually in conflict with his inclinations).[29] The true moral motive becomes doing something because it is your duty. Doing your duty by accident or from a selfish motive is right, but only doing duty for its own sake makes it moral.[30] One must remember that moral judgements are only one type of legitimate judgement. We can praise a person as amiable or reliable, and action as useful or friendly; praising something as moral requires different criteria.

Yet a moral principle must, as we have seen, be obeyed for its own sake it must contain its own authority. Kant makes this point sharply by contrasting categorical and hypothetical imperatives.[31] A hypothetical imperative can be technical or prudential, the former being advice about the way to achieve any chosen goal, the latter about goals such as health or happiness, which we take for granted. When such an imperative is fully spelled out, the goal is expressed in an 'if' clause: If you want to go to Birmingham, take the train on platform five. If you want to be understood, write simple sentences. If you want to keep your health, don't overeat. In many cases, for example when a student is told to read a particular text, the 'if' clause which contains the reason for the action proposed is suppressed because already understood.

In a categorical imperative no reason for the imperative is specified; this is the form which moral rules must take. 'Be honest' is such a rule, but the moment you add 'if you want to keep out of jail' it ceases to be moral and becomes prudential advice. (You can, of course, always add 'if you want to be moral' without abandoning the moral status of the imperative, but that gives no more an independent reason than saying 'Get up if you want to be up'.)

So what is morality all about if it is required neither for our happiness nor for the smooth running of society? In any ordinary sense, it does not serve any purpose at all. Now why should we then obey the voice of reason when it issues moral commands. Could we not equally side with our instincts and animal cravings against an (apparently) tyrannical reason? After all, we have already confirmed that whatever aim we may have, be it safe roads or stable marriages, could be achieved without bringing morality into play. And yet something, we feel, is achieved when people are faithful or considerate because they think it right rather than because of fear or calculation. It constitutes moral worth, but why strive for it?

In one sense, as Kant explains, there can be no answer. If we have reached fundamental principles, we cannot explain them by reference to more fundamental ones without denying that they were fundamental in the first place.[32] If Kant is right, it lies in the nature of reason to be the source of ultimate principles, be it in the theoretical or the practical sphere. It is as meaningless to ask what gives reason the power and right to control our practical actions as to ask the same question about the way we use mathematical principles and impose a causal order on nature. We certainly accept the autonomy of reason in the latter sphere, for who would dream of asking what on earth made someone conclude that two plus two makes four? Practical reason, according to Kant, speaks to us even more directly than theoretical reason, for while the latter presupposes a context of experience, the former speaks clearly even to the ignorant and inexperienced.[33]

Nevertheless Kant provides a further explanation for choosing to obey the voice of reason. Obviously there can be no appeal to an independent arbiter between reason and passion. But choosing to be moral, and so submitting himself to principles of his own reason, man asserts his membership in the realm of reason and thereby his dignity.[34] As an animal and part of nature, he is in bondage to causal laws; as a moral agent, he is free. The paradox that we must talk about man as, on the one hand, determined by physical, psychological, and social factors and, on the other, self-determining is highly relevant to sociology; we shall return to it.

Only one final point remains to be made about Kant's moral philosophy. The formality of a purely rational moral principle has struck many readers as arid and remote from life, but this is, at least partly, a misunderstanding. Kant makes it perfectly clear that making a specific choice involves all kinds of empirical information. Before we can translate our love for a neighbour into practical, effective action we have to discover what he is like and what he needs, what we can do and what the circumstances are like. Some of this we know from everyday experience, some we may learn from the social sciences; other information required may be scientific or technological. Kant discussed some of these matters in his writings but insisted that they can be clearly distinguished from the moral principles which alone can provide the ultimate reason for action.[35] You can know that someone needed help which you can provide and yet say So what? unless your reason tells you that the universality principle requires you to give help, if you would want help in a similar situation.

This account of Kant's moral philosophy is, like the one of his epistemology, selective and omits some of its interesting features. However, the brief discussion of man as a partially rational being capable of directing himself by rules of his making, free because subject to a moral law, but at the same time in bondage to nature, sufficiently prepares the ground for a discussion of Kant's relevance for sociology.

The Philosophy of Science

First and foremost Kant affected sociology through his enormous influence on all our views about the nature and provenance of knowledge. By reflecting critically on the long development of science which had culminated in the work of Newton, he inspired subsequent philosophies of science. The great forward leap of science in the sixteenth and seventeenth centuries had rested on explicit discussions of the scientific method, in which it was made clear that science can confine itself neither to gathering facts nor to speculating in the void, but must base itself on a judicious combination of observation and thought. Kant entered on the question about the precise relation between experience and thought more deeply than anyone before or after him. His analysis has remained paradigmatic for our views of what can be meaningfully asserted about the world and how theorising is related to observation.

Several important consequences for sociology follow from the delicate balance Kant struck when he postulated the creative activity of the mind in cognition and yet insisted that in the process the mind encountered something independently given from outside. He clearly sided with empiricism against rationalism by stressing that reason unsupported by experience 'flapped its wings impotently in the void'.[36] Yet like the rationalists, and unlike the empiricists, he maintained the importance of theoretical speculation. Precisely for this reason he is more convincing than rationalists or empiricists in pressing the claims of abstract thought on the one side, and warning against speculation unsupported by evidence on the other. Both aspects are relevant for sociology.

The idea that in cognition we are in contact, however indirectly, with an ultimate and unyielding reality, though commonsensical enough, raises a difficult point in Kant's philosophy, because some of his presuppositions make this idea precarious. For one thing, we can never catch the data transmitted to us in their raw state; to try to see what they are like before they have been transformed by our own cognitive apparatus is like turning on the light to see what the dark looks like. Furthermore Kant had denied that we could know anything about ultimate reality and had therefore debarred himself from asserting that it was capable of affecting our senses. On grounds such as these, idealist philosophers, Hegel among them, had eliminated the idea that knowledge involves something alien impinging on the mind. Yet whatever the difficulties and the at least apparent inconsistencies of his theory, Kant was, I believe, right to retain the sense that something exists outside us, and to leave us with what Kierkegaard called 'the sting of the real'. Once we accept that thought is creative and even subject to arbitrary conventions of our own making, it becomes all the more important, if we are not to succumb to a subjectivism which dissolves reality into a dream, to insist that there is something which resists some interpretations and determines what we think and how we speak about it. The danger of subjectivism is particularly acute if we abandon, as we may well do, Kant's second line of defence, namely the conviction that we are all subject to the same rules for acquiring knowledge.

Insisting on the importance of thought is as necessary as insisting on the need for evidence. The impressions we receive, the experience we gain, certainly must be taken seriously, but they may mislead unless critically examined. Recording one's own impressions or putting down what others tell us is not sociology. Unless we are guided by a theoretical framework, we will be too credulous about our data and too sloppy in our interpretations of them. As Kant insisted, research means asking pertinent questions, not just looking. To be intelligent and to the point, such questions must spring from theories which define what we want or need to know, how we can check our findings, and how we can combine them with other information into a consistent whole.

With the ponderous wit and massive common sense so characteristic of him, Kant warns us of the futility of posing questions which are absurd either because they are not theoretically justified or because they call for meaningless answers not based on experience: 'It is a great and necessary proof of wisdom and sagacity to know what questions may be reasonably asked. For if a question is absurd in itself and calls for an answer where there is no answer, it does not only throw disgrace on the questioner, but often tempts an incautious listener into absurd answers, thus presenting, as the ancients said, the spectacle of one person milking a he-goat, and the other holding a sieve.'[37]

Three issues of special interest to students of sociology arise from Kant's epistemology. One of these concerns the degree of scepticism justified in the face of the kind of evidence sociologists must deal with. At a first glance it appears that Kant would have sided with, and has lent his support to, the positivistically inclined sociologists who insist on such 'hard' data as the observation of external behaviour. However, a different answer emerges if we take into account his whole style of approach, rather than particular arguments. We have seen that again and again, in the case of theoretical knowledge as well as of morality, Kant did not ask if we possessed knowledge but accepted the voice of common sense and then proceeded to justify it. He would, therefore, not have dreamed of excluding consideration of man's mental life on dogmatic grounds, as do extreme behaviourists. Instead he would have accepted that we do know what other people feel and considered how this feat is possible.

The other two issues are related to each other and arise from Kant's belief that the mind is active in cognition. The first of these is that by drawing attention to the need for sociological theorising, and for recognising that experience is already 'theory-laden', the belief in active cognition emphasises the fact that human beings invariably theorise. The sociologist must therefore theorise about theories. Indeed the matter gets even more involved. Today sociology has become sufficiently popularised to colour the way ordinary people interpret their own experiences. Then the sociologist sees—like Narcissus looking into the pool—

his own image, or more precisely the reflection of his own theories, when he questions people about their views. The sociologist's methodology must take account of these facts, and Kant's
epistemology helps him do so.

The third issue which arises from Kant's theory of knowledge
is that his idea that the mind imposes its own perspectives and
presuppositions on what it comes to know opens the door to
the sociology of knowledge. Once we accept that knowledge is
not a simple matter of something imprinting itself on the mind,
it becomes possible to consider if and to what extent the patterns
we impose on experience are socially conditioned. The Copernican Revolution, which shook the foundations of philosophy,
shattered traditional theology, and inspired a new confidence
among poets, also prepared the way for an important and interesting development in sociology: the study of knowledge itself, as a social product.

Kant himself did not travel down the road of a sociology of
knowledge, because he believed that the fundamental categories
which the mind employs are timeless and universal. He was
interested in the laws of thought and the fundamental principles
of morality rather than in the changing, socially determined rules
which govern languages, social conventions, or legal enact-
ments. Whether Kant was right about singling out some fundamental principles as being beyond social change is still being
debated. For example, both the theories that language is entirely
conventional and that all languages share a 'fundamental gram-
mar' have their advocates today.[38]

Kant clung to the idea of universally valid categories because
the alternative would have led him into circular arguments and
made the objectivity of knowledge, as well as of morality, un-
tenable. There is something to be said for his case, because
reason must be autonomous if it is to constitute man's capacity
to think cogently and to produce principles and concepts which
enable us to coordinate our impressions and shape them into
knowledge. If my conclusion that two plus two is four, or that
the readings of the thermometer indicates a fall in temperature,
could be entirely due to a stomachache, or being middle-class,
rather than to the thought processes leading up to the conclusion, then we would have to cease speaking of knowledge al-

together. Only if a chain of reasoning has gone wrong may we ask about the outside forces which interfered with it.

Kant's belief in timeless categories sets strict limits to a sociology of knowledge but does not eliminate the case for it. Indeed, his philosophy indirectly encouraged the idea that man's intellectual life was socially and historically conditioned. Up to the beginning of the nineteenth century, students of human nature and the social world had emphasised unvarying features and persisting patterns in their subject. By the turn of the century, interest grew in historical change and the differences between different communities. Kant himself was not particularly interested in this matter and did not inspire the new enthusiasm for it. One must not underestimate, though, the significance of the fact that his intellectual revolution *made sense* of the new attitude. If knowledge is simply the imprint of nature on us, and morality simply the word of God, then whatever is socially variable is just a frill. If on the other hand the mind constructs its world, there is no reason why it should not reconstruct its own rules and categories or why interaction of different minds—that is, social context—should not play a major part in this.

In fact, many of Kant's followers have taken this line and argued that our whole system of concepts, embodied in languages, myths, religions, and art, and not a few timeless categories, represent the rules and patterns which we superimpose on experience.[39] As these are unquestionably historical and social products, they can be subjected to a sociology of knowledge, even though they may contain a timeless core which makes, for example, translation from one language to another possible.

The picture of man as endowed with an active mind and capable of theorising which emerges from Kant's epistemology is expanded in his moral philosophy. His description of human rationality, which is central in his approach, deserves the sociologist's special attention. Kant basically defined reason as the faculty of rules, that is, man's capacity to produce rules and arrange his thinking and acting according to them. Nothing picks out man's unique endowment more sharply or points more incisively to a subject which sociologists cannot ignore, because it is fraught with consequences for their methodology. When we study natural phenomena such as falling stones, we try to establish laws which are, basically, generalisations about the uniform way objects fall. Many of the uniformities in human behaviour cannot be accounted for in this manner. The highway code is not a generalisation of how motorists usually drive; unlike laws of nature it influences rather than describes behaviour, must be known if it is to be effective, and can be changed, defied, or broken. A rule can obviously be used to explain behaviour, but not in the way in which the law of gravity explains the fall of stones.

Man's capacity to use reason technically and to choose means towards ends rationally is also methodologically significant. Though we frequently and for many reasons do not use this capacity, we undoubtedly possess it. Even the most fanatical irrationalists or exponents of man's close relationship to other animals would not deny this. If it matters to me to be in New York tomorrow and only a plane will get me there in time, then flying is the rational choice. If I choose it, no more explanation is required than in the case of my concluding that two plus two is four. Only my failure to make this choice needs further explaining.

Applying the inherent tendency of reason towards consistency, system, and the imposition of rules to the pursuit of practical aims is an extension of technical reason. It is widely assumed that such an approach serves efficiency, whatever the aim and the specific means required for its achievement. A factory, an office, or a government works better if there are general rules, rather than day-by-day decisions, about who does what, when people should arrive, when they are to be paid, or whom they should make their complaints to. Even individuals who can arrange their own time are usually more efficient if they regularise when to get up, have their meals, or do their work. The nature of such technical rules and their role in social life are obvious topics for sociological study.

Technical reason can be contrasted to theoretical reason as 'practical', because it guides action rather than cognition. Strictly speaking, however, it is not practical reason, because something other than reason actually prompts the action. My motive for flying is the desire to get to New York; my motive for arranging a factory more rationally is to make it more profitable; reason

only tells me *how* to achieve my aims. For reason to be truly
practical it must determine choice in the sense in which moral
principles do. This idea of reason as a source of morality draws
the sociologist's attention to topics he ignores at his peril.

No one is likely to disagree with Kant's view that man is a
creature constantly pulled by instincts and passions. By he also
believed, more controversially, that reason has a pull of its own.
Its demand for consistency extends beyond theoretical and technical concerns and gives rise to principles of action which owe
nothing to experience or training. One can say even to a child,
once it has begun to be rational, 'If you do not want other
children to trample on your toys, surely it is wrong to trample
on theirs,' and trust that he will appreciate the force of the
argument.

The relationship of sociology to a moral philosophy like that
of Kant raises a number of questions. Are moral issues relevant
to sociology? Are philosophical and sociological accounts of human choices in conflict with each other or compatible, and if the
latter, to what extent? Can the sociologist be morally neutral,
and if not, what should he do about it? The answer to the first
question is straightforward enough. Moral issues, however the
sociologist may ultimately interpret them, form a prominent part
of his subject matter. 'The Protestant ethic', 'New England Puritanism', 'the moral teaching of the Catholic Church', 'the work
ethic'—all these, as well as more specific moral ideas such as
family loyalty or fairness, have played a part in sociological accounts, because social conflicts, political controversies, and historical changes often revolve around them.

It can also be seen that moral philosophy can fulfill the essential role of defining the nature of these issues. Laying down
moral rules, discussing them, and conforming to them are social
activities, but that does not distinguish them from devising and
obeying conventions or rules of etiquette. It is only their claim
to be rational and universally binding which gives them their
unique character. A similar point can be made about religion or
science; they are social activities, but would not be what we
think they are if they were *only* social activities. Each has an
extra dimension which can be explored, but not by sociology.
Though essentially negative, this point is enormously important,

because if sociologists ignore it and instead work on the basis that these different spheres of human life are not what they claim to be, all sociology becomes a kind of debunking, or looking behind the various masks and human illusions. But if religion is nothing but the opium of the masses, what distinguishes it from television as the opium of the masses or, for that matter, opium as the opium of the masses? In Hegel's famous phrase, 'the night descends in which all cows are black'.

If Kant's philosophical analysis thus protects sociology from playing *Hamlet* without the prince, it also leaves room for, and indeed requires, sociological knowledge both for moral action and for the understanding of moral principles. Concrete moral guidance (unlike the pure moral principle) obviously must take account of social facts as socially determined and relative to particular societies. If there is a moral obligation for a bank manager, let us say, not to quit his job without notice, it exists because the man has a particular job in a particular institution at a particular time and place. All this is a product of social forces and can be sociologically explained.

There remains however, if Kant is right, a moral core which is independent of these conditions and equally essential. Without it, a man may recognise the social situation he finds himself in and yet see no reason why it should impose a moral obligation on him. This distinction between a moral core and a socially determined husk also accounts for the variety of moral beliefs and practices in different societies, which has sometimes given rise to moral scepticism. The belief of some societies that it is right to have several wives, or eat one's grandmother, may well be due to their different social circumstances and traditions or to their views—sometimes mistaken—as to what things are like and what is good for people, and not to any difference in their basic moral conviction about our duties to others. If, however, they do differ fundamentally, we can judge them in the light of Kant's criteria. Fear of ethnocentricity or cultural arrogance and dedication to scholarly detachment has made us, at times, too afraid of taking sides.

A final issue which arises very acutely in the context of Kant's philosophy is that of human freedom. The conception of man as free carries implications for the extent to which sociological explanations are possible, and what form they must take. Once we accept that there is such a thing as morality, we must also accept that there is freedom. Moral rules would be meaningless, and moral condemnation absurd, if people were never free: 'ought' implies 'can'.[40] If I tell a boy he ought to improve his work or punish him for not having done so, I assume that he is capable of pulling himself together, stopping his laziness, and doing better. If the quality of his work were entirely determined by heredity or social environment, it would be useless and cruel to blame him for it.

However, accepting human freedom raises the question how it can be reconciled with a causal order of nature. Common sense accepts that we are all shaped by the past, by our heredity and the impact of our physical and social environment. The behaviour of his parents, the attitude of his companions, and the prevailing customs of the society around him all shape the personality of a child. Unless we accept this, psychology and sociology, and any other systematic study of man, would be impossible. We could never draw conclusions about the connection between events, never arrive at generalisations, never predict what would be the likely outcome of an activity. Even moral actions themselves would become meaningless, unless we concede that such knowledge and such predictions are possible. How could it be my duty, for example, to arrange for an orphan to go to a foster home, unless I believed that a home background was likely to provide him with a happier life and a better preparation for the future?

A theory about human freedom need not assume indeterminacy, because free actions are determined by the agent's own thought. That is why free rational action does not, in itself, present a particular problem about prediction. Yet this does not resolve the problem of accounting for the paradox that actions are both free (in the sense of being determined by the agent's reflections) and determined by the past and outside factors. Kant's solution to this problem differs from Spinoza's because it hinges on the distinction between the knowing 'I' and the empirical self which Kant established in his epistemology.[41] It is the empirical self which is part of the phenomenal world and therefore subject to causal laws in terms of which it can be explained, while the

knowing 'I', lying outside the empirical world and only revealed
by a transcendental deduction, can be free because it is not
subject to laws (like that of causality) which we impose on our
experience in the act of cognition.

Kant does not provide convincing reasons why the 'I' presupposed in cognition should also be the moral self. The theory
remains an assumption and, in any case, like most philosophic
theories about freedom, does not provide an immediately convincing solution. Surely, we might say, a man either stops drink-
ing because he made a moral choice *or* because his past
conditioned him to do so. We cannot have it both ways. In order
to make sense of Kant's solution it is useful to make use of the
metaphor of the dramatist-actor. Performing in his own play he
is, as actor, determined by the script, but as the author he is the
free originator of what he says and does. Analogies of this kind
cannot be taken too far and do not clinch any argument. Kant's
theory of the two selves—the absolute, spontaneous 'I' of cognition and moral choice, and the empirical, physically embodied,
and socially moulded person—remains difficult and leaves many
questions unanswered. One of the most important ones concerns the relation between the two selves, which the dramatist-
actor metaphor illustrates but does not explain. Because the cognitive 'I' is not empirically knowable, its relation to anything
else must remain obscure. The idea is, however, absorbingly
interesting and potentially fruitful. If we think, for example, of
the cognitive 'I' as the core of personality around which layers
of socialisation form the outward personality, we have the germ
of a hypothesis—in fact the kind of hypothesis used by G. H.
Mead.[42]

In any case, Kant's theory makes it clear that in talking about
freedom and causal order respectively, we are adopting different
points of view which, though irreconcilable in any simple way,
are both unavoidable, because the sociologist cannot for a moment assign freedom to the lumber room of speculation and
concentrate on the causal order of events. A sociological analysis
of human activities should not ignore such notions as account-
ability or responsibility, which means regarding someone not
only as the cause of an event, but also as causing the event
freely. If he too were completely determined by external causes,

the idea of responsibility would dissolve. If a young man blamed his father for his own actions, that father could, in turn, attribute the way he brought up his son to the grandfather's influence. The grandfather, if death had not closed his mouth, would refer responsibility back to more distant ancestors until we arrived at the sociological equivalent of original sin. Only a conception of freedom like the one developed by Kant can protect us from this kind of absurdity.

Personal liberty and responsibility are not the only issues for students of society to consider among the possible limitations of complete determinism. Human life is—we assume—creative and produces new things not accountable by the extrapolation of causal chains. True, the seasons keep on following each other in much the same way, 'birth, copulation, and death' continue to be part of man's existence, crises and wars recur, and people complain today about the younger generation much as they did in ancient Greece. Yet the claim that 'there is nothing new under the sun' cannot be taken literally. So much, from the new technology to a new poem or play, cannot be predicted, for to predict tomorrow's poetry or inventions would be to write those poems or to make those inventions. The same applies to the social changes and new institutions which are the products of human choice. Only an intellectual framework which leaves room both for social conditioning and for the spontaneous creation of new things can make sense of our social reality.

Kant's picture of man is complex and controversial, yet it goes a long way to account for the bewildering fact that we cannot but think of man as a creature physically and socially determined yet morally free, the object of knowledge yet the creator of all knowledge, the product of the past and yet the architect of a new future, a product of society yet responsible for its shortcomings.

6 • *Conclusion*: The Theme of Reason in Modern Sociology

Three questions dominate current debates about the role of reason. What is the range of problems reason can solve? How rational is man? And how can reason provide and guarantee knowledge of the world? Applied to sociology, these questions take a more specific form. What is the scope of sociology? How are we to conceive its subject matter? And what are its appropriate methods? The philosophy of reason has its own answers to these questions, and to review them in the context of contemporary concerns may help to bring out their continuing relevance.

The Scope of Reason

The first question can be more fully spelled out as follows. Is reason confined to solving theoretical and technical problems, or can it also help us to discover or at least clarify final goals and principles of conduct? Pointed directly towards sociology, this becomes the question whether the study of society can achieve more than a contribution to man's growing control and mastery of his environment. Such technical control is undoubtedly needed, because some of the misery and conflict of our time can be attributed to our managing social, industrial, and international relations inefficiently. There is little doubt that sociology can help in this, though there is room for improvement. Studying how things actually work in the social world can tell us how to make them work better; it can already give us useful advice about spreading information effectively, or encouraging particular political attitudes by creating a favourable social environment. Though we may have occasional misgivings about being purely manipulative towards people, we welcome, on the whole, the improvement and use of social techniques for whatever goals we may have in mind. Some sociologists are content with this role, but others think that sociology has a contribution to make towards judging the goals themselves. Aware that philosophers are faltering in their traditional job of examining moral ideals, these sociologists wonder if it is up to them to fill the gap. The story of how we reached this point is an intriguing part of our intellectual history.

A curious dialectic has been at work in driving reason into retreat. Confidence in reason provided the ethos and intellectual climate which made the development of science possible. The spectacular theoretical and practical results achieved by scientific advance made science appear to be the highest and purest realisation of rationality. From there it was only a step to argue, as some philosophers, particularly those described as positivists, have done, that *only* what is scientifically demonstrable is rationally acceptable. But once we make the scientific process into the sole paradigm for the achievement of knowledge, we are forced to conclude that moral and political, let alone aesthetic, judgements are not rational and that philosophy itself lies outside the sphere of reason.

The consequences of this view are serious, for some people conclude that if moral and political judgements are not scientific, and therefore not rational, they are ill-founded. There is then no reason to value charity above mass murder, or democracy above fascism. No rational discussion is possible between people who differ on social or political issues, and only force, bribery, or brainwashing can change peoples' minds. The process of dissolution goes further: once we maintain that only science is rational, we end up having to admit—as some philosophers of science have done—that even science is not rational, because it rests, as can be shown, on philosophic presuppositions.

Philosophers, like Husserl, who pitted their arguments against this rising tide of irrationalism conducted little more than a rearguard action.[1] What was needed to take the wind out of the positivists' sails was to show that scientific procedures, or procedures very much like them, could provide objective answers to moral and political questions. Sociology seemed tailor-made for this role and therefore became the residual heir of philosophy once it had become discredited. Sociologists who patiently examine what man is like, what he is capable of, and how he functions in society and suffers in history should, it was felt, be able to tell us something about how man should live and what he is meant to be. Admittedly common sense and philosophy agree that moral judgements do not follow directly from any facts. The fact, for example, that a lot of people do something, want to do it, are happier for doing it, or even think it right, does not make it right. Nevertheless it seems reasonable that those who occupy themselves 'scientifically' with human life, its needs, aspirations, and dangers, might have something to say about its meaning and appropriate goals. So sociologists, as well as a wider public, have come to look to sociology as a source of guidance.

This tendency is encouraged by the fact that sociology is full of terms which carry an evaluative meaning, which helps sociologists to have their cake and eat it (that is, be objective and morally significant at the same time). 'Normal', 'natural', 'functional', 'dysfunctional', 'anomy', and 'alienation' are such value-laden terms, for who would wish to be alienated, prefer the dysfunctional to the functional, or deplore something that is normal? Some sociologists are absentminded or even a little shamefaced about this; others accept it as a proper part of their work. Certainly Marxist-oriented sociologists are among the latter, for one of the appeals of dialectical materialism has always been its claim to provide scientifically based guidance. But this interpretation of sociology is by no means confined to them. Edward Shils, for example, wrote that 'sociological analysis is a continuation in a contemporary idiom of the great efforts of the human mind to render judgement on man's vicissitudes on earth', and Tom Burns said, 'The practice of sociology is criticism: to criticise or to raise questions about claims and assumptions concerning the value or meaning of conduct and achievement'.[2]

Statements like these, clearly, ask of sociology much more than painstaking accuracy. and come down against Max Weber's famous 'value neutrality'.[3] Indeed, many sociologists not only think it impossible to obey Weber's injunction to refrain from taking sides in their work but think that doing so constitutes a betrayal, a 'treason of the clerks' which opens the door to moral nihilism. This point is clearly made in Laurie Taylor's review of A. W. Gouldner's *The Coming Crisis of Western Sociology:* 'Sociologists, more than any other academics, must declare which side they are on. For it is they who have so often claimed to know what was best for society in the past, it is they who now dispense social prescriptions to government and industry as well as to students and public.'[4] If these claims mean anything it is that sociologists can and should draw moral conclusions from their knowledge of social life. This is indeed 'a continuation in a modern idiom' of the debate about the role and scope of reason.

In one sense there is no conflict between these two roles of sociology, the one concerned with means, the other with ends; one might even say that they complement each other. A sociology concerned with the ends of social life can profit from knowledge of the means to achieve them; indeed, information about the means available for different lines of action may even help to clarify these ends. On the other hand a sociology which seeks knowledge and skill but not moral illumination cannot properly get hold of its subject matter without becoming aware of moral issues. Max Weber makes this point, though in his view the evaluation of the moral issues themselves must take place outside sociology.

> Only a small portion of existing concrete reality is coloured by our value-conditioned interest and it alone is significant to us. It is significant because it reveals relationships which are important to us due to their connection with our values. Only because and to the extent that this is the case is it worthwhile for us to know it in its individual features. We cannot discover, however, what is meaningful to us by means of a 'presuppositionless' investigation of empirical data. Rather perception of its meaningfulness to us is the presupposition of its becoming an *object* of investigation.[5]

Yet a sociology of means and a sociology of ends are not wholly compatible, because each involves a different attitude to its subject matter. As long as we treat sociology as a technical subject, the investigator can remain detached, ignoring or taking his own values for granted as beyond or above the matter in hand. He can deal with people and their actions much as scientists deal with the behaviour of liquids or gases. But the moment he enters into the content of human goals, his own presuppositions and valuations confront those of the people he studies. He is no longer looking at an object in front of him, but at fellow human beings with whom he shares common human problems. When his judgements conflict with those of the people he studies, the question of subjectivity arises, for being a sociologist does not entitle him to think that his views are automatically superior to those of others. When he seeks to justify them, he cannot help but notice that others too have reasons for their views. It would be insufferably arrogant to assume that his Marxism (or liberalism) is rationally based while the liberalism (or Marxism) of those he studies is merely a reflection of their social background. Confronted by a multiplicity of prima facie, equally valid points of view, the sociologist is forced to question his subject radically, which in turn raises critical methodological questions.

Human Rationality

The second major issue at the heart of current debates, the nature of man, is as revelant for the theme of reason as it is for sociology. The question of man's rationality is doubly significant for the sociologist, because it concerns on the one hand the nature of his subject matter, and on the other his own capacity for exploring it. An investigator mapping out the lines of his research must make some preliminary assumptions about his subject—draw, as it were, a preliminary picture of it. For the sociologist this subject is man, with specific reference to his rationality which makes language, knowledge, and highly organised social life possible. This same rationality enables the investigator to understand his subject, assess his material, and theorise about it; if we are to assure the reliability of our research we must look critically at rationality itself.

The fact that in sociology man studies man, serves the ideal of self-knowledge and offers the advantages of closeness and familiarity, but makes objectivity difficult. A dangerous circle may be involved if we make the same assumptions about our subject that we do about our capacities for knowing it. Any initial bias may narrow or distort our conclusions and leave us with a conception of reality which we have superimposed in accordance with our predilections.

Though there is no foolproof way to avoid error or self-deception, we can do something to minimise the risk by examining closely what a preliminary concept of man must be like to meet our requirements. This kind of examination is a traditional part of philosophy, but in the last few decades it has developed into a separate discipline with a name of its own: philosophic anthropology.[6] The German philosopher and sociologist Max Scheler, who coined the term, made its function clear: 'The real philosophic task [was] the establishment of a philosophic anthropology that would transcend the relativity of specific historically and socially located viewpoints.'[7] Among philosophers and sociologists who agree on this issue, D. H. Wrong makes the point particularly vigorously and links it with a warning about the dangers of an insufficiently critical conception of man: 'I do not see how, at the level of theory, sociologists can fail to make assumptions about human nature. If our assumptions are left implicit, we will inevitably presuppose a view of man that is tailor-made to our special needs; when our sociological theory over-stresses the stability and integration of society we will end up imagining that man is the disembodied conscience-driven, status-seeking phantom of current theory.'[8]

Philosophic anthropology produces a blueprint rather than a photograph of human nature. It produces an outline which is neither a substitute for, nor a product of, empirical research and needs to be filled in. To prevent such a sketch from being a mere speculative fantasy it must be devised as the answer to the following questions: What is actually presupposed when we think ourselves capable of knowing anything? What aspects of human nature must we assume to exist before we can begin our studies? Do our studies of man fulfil our requirements, and if not, could they be made more successful by a revision of our presuppositions about man? For example, we do not learn by research that man is capable of knowledge, because we would not have set out to study the matter if we had not assumed our capacity for it all along. Likewise we assume, rather than discover, that human beings can form purposes, for in observing a person or a group we ask, Is *this* behaviour purposeful? not Is any behaviour purposeful? Other assumptions are not as unchallengeable. For example, assumptions about human nature have ranged from its being completely fixed to its being infinitely malleable.[9] In such cases one must consider how far an assumption tallies with other assumptions, or various findings, and how far it encourages promising lines of research.

Philosophic anthropology also helps, as Max Scheler stipulates, to overcome the difficulties raised by social and historical relativity. Unless we can assume that underlying the numerous differences between human beings there are universal features, we would have no common subject matter about which to make generalisations, and no bridge between people divided by temperament, culture, and social background. It is difficult for modern Englishmen to understand ancient Romans, for Europeans to understand Africans, old people the young, or the rich the poor; without a basis of common humanity it would be impossible.

In addition philosophic anthropology provides a model which helps us to frame (or discard) hypotheses about human life and society. There are, for example, two well-known alternative conceptions of man (both sketched in Plato's *Republic*) which lead to alternative conceptions of society. One is that man is essentially selfish, so that society results either from one faction imposing its will on another,[10] or from a compromise by which everyone is forced to forgo some of his aspirations and receives in return a measure of security.[11] The other conception is that man is essentially a social being who can only fulfil himself properly in society. If any proof were needed that such an issue cannot be settled by reference to the facts, it is provided by the continued existence of both these views. In the context of industry, for instance, some people argue to this day that there must be a conflict of interest between workers and managers or owners over sharing the profits, while others are convinced that both have a common interest in maximising production by co-operation and thus assuring a bigger share for everyone.

Less controversial is the assumption we are likely to make about any society, however alien or primitive: that it possesses a system of language because the capacity for language is a universal human characteristic. For the same reason the use of linguistic expressions as evidence can be assumed to be methodologically proper and important, and one can give short shrift to any theory which recommends avoiding such evidence because it is not available in other disciplines.

By pointing to such features as man's capacity for language or knowledge, philosophic anthropology makes explicit what everyone knows and accepts. In other cases, such as that of man's sociability, it pinpoints controversial issues. The extent of man's rationality is undoubtedly one of these. Is his reason merely 'the slave of the passions',[12] or can it be a judge of his goals? We can see how the same theme recurs whether we talk of reason in general, of sociology, or of human nature.

Methodology

On the third issue we have listed, that of methodology, related questions arise, for how we proceed must be coloured by our conception of what sociology is about and what man is like. Any conclusion about methodology will in turn be reflected in our views of these other topics. *How* we conduct our research must have a bearing on what we think of sociology and what conclusions we draw about man.

Methodology takes up the theme of reason in two ways. Firstly, it explores reason as an instrument, asking how various thought processes like deduction, comparison, generalisation, and theorising can contribute to the achievement of knowledge. The distinction between logical rules of inference and principles for discovering something new (of which Descartes's analytical method is an example) come under this heading. Secondly, methodology uses reason as a judge of all methods, by weighing the rigour, epistemological soundness, and fruitfulness of different approaches. Particularly important is to judge how appropriate a method is to a particular subject. Within sociology this is a live issue, because some sociologists are anxious to use the same scientific methods which have proved of value in the sciences, while others want to limit the use of such methods because they cannot do justice to the unique features of the human world.[13]

How far, we may ask, are we entitled to look for philosophical foundations of methodology? In the first resort, methods, even if they are defined as general lines of approach and not specific techniques, must be chosen and developed by the experts in the fields to which they are to be applied. Yet though they cannot be intelligently discussed without expertise, methods rest ultimately on our general view of reality and of the capacity we have for knowing it, in other words, on a philosophical framework which only metaphysics, philosophic anthropology, and epistemology can provide. This framework itself must be adjustable, not only through philosophical argument but in the light of evidence as to how successful particular methods turn out to be. The way philosophical theory and practical success influence each other can be easily illustrated. If anyone suggested that a weather forecast was based on examining the entrails of chickens, we would be suspicious and even scornful, because our view of the world does not allow for an intelligible connection between the two. Yet if gazing at chicken entrails consistently produced forecasts superior to those made by other methods, it would become reasonable to reexamine the general assumptions which fail to make sense of this success.

The first specific question about reason in methodology concerns the importance of theory in the collection of data. Some sociologists proceed as if the facts spoke for themselves, and concentrate on collecting information and evaluating it statistically. However, the view that facts are theory-laden predominates. Early in the history of modern social science, Auguste Comte had already noted that 'no real observation of any kind of phenomena is possible, except insofar as it is first directed, and finally interpreted, by some theory,'[14] and more recently Erving Goffmann went so far as to suggest that 'a loose, speculative approach to a fundamental area of conduct is better than a rigorous blindness to it.'[15] Gunnar Myrdal put it most explicitly: 'Scientific facts do not exist *per se*, waiting to be discovered by scientists. A scientific fact is a construction abstracted from a complex and interwoven reality by means of arbitrary definitions and classifications.'[16] These quotations, to which similar ones could be added, indicate a widespread readiness to see reason as capable of advancing ahead of experience and imposing its patterns upon it.

We must also ask how far such theorising is justified by assumptions about a rational order in the subject matter. A causal order is the most obvious assumption which sociologists share with common sense and the various sciences. When there is an increase in delinquency or illegitimate births, the sociologist will assume without the slightest hesitation that such a change can be accounted for in terms of a circumstance, or combination of circumstances, which preceded and precipitated it. The concept of functional structures is also used in sociology (as it is in biology) but is more controversial, because it presupposes purposes on the part of individuals or nature. To attribute purposes to nature, society, or any entity of this kind is highly speculative, and the moment we rely on the purposes of individuals for our sociological explanations, problems about subjective meaning arise. Wanting to know what X wants, and why, raises new methodological problems; in order to avoid them, positivists try to interpret function in causal terms as far as possible. 'But', as John Rex wrote, 'within the positivist tradition functional as distinct from causal explanation presents something of an embarrassment.'[17] The problem is, of course, as Rex (following W. W. Isajiw) points out, that it is necessary to attribute causal efficacy not only to events but to 'the need of a system'.

Over and above a causal and functional order we may also attribute to the human world an order which completely distinguishes it from anything else in the world, namely its being permeated by mind or spirit. By this I do not mean anything more mysterious than the presence of culture in the anthropologist's sense of the word. Language, works of art, laws, institutions, and traditions present men with relatively stable order which is the product of man's activity and, though not exclusively the product of reason, contains rational structures. Hegel and his followers called it 'objective mind', K. R. Popper 'the third world',[18] but in the present context it is best to let a sociologist, Émile Durkheim, speak about it: 'the individual at least obscurely takes account of the fact that above his private ideas, there is a world of absolute ideas according to which he must shape his own; he catches a glimpse of a whole intellectual kingdom in which he participates, but which is greater than he.'[19]

One thing stands out about these various ways in which the human world is structured. They are tangibly present in human life, while their existence, if postulated about reality at large, is highly speculative and controversial. We can never experience how one billiard ball propels another (only that the one rolls first, and then the other), but we do experience how an insult *makes* us angry. We certainly form purposes and judge how particular objects can serve them, even if the universe has no overall purpose and is not a functionally arranged cosmos. The human world is certainly structured by ideas whether that is true of the universe as a whole or not.

There is a further distinctive characteristic of the human world: in it individual entities and their relations to each other are important and provide focal points for explaining social reality. That sociology deals with individual groups, organisations, trades, institutions, and societies raises a question about the rationality of its approach, because the widely accepted norm of science is to produce generalisations and seek general laws. Can the study of individuals be as intellectually respectable as the search for uniformities, or, to use Heinrich Richert's famous terms, can an 'ideographic' approach be as legitimate as a 'nomothetic' one?[20]

There is certainly nothing mysterious about the former, because we use it in everyday life as well as in the sciences when we explain or account for an individual thing in terms of its relations to other individual things. I can quite reasonably say that my left foot hurts because there is a stone in my shoe or that the seasons are determined by the position of the earth relative to the sun. Particularly significant among explanations of this kind are those which refer to parts and wholes, as in a statement that a certain club has a bad reputation because its members are ruffians or that someone knows how to deal with people because he is a member of a large family. The evidence that sociology very largely deals with a part/whole relationship is overwhelming. Two quotations on the matter will suffice. John

Madge said in a talk on Sociology and Social Problems Today, 'Sociology is the study of the interacting groups of which our society is composed',[21] Lucien Goldmann wrote, "Here [in the human sciences] the progress of knowledge proceeds . . . through a continual oscillation between the whole and its parts."[22]

But far from being exclusive alternatives, the ideographic and nomothetic approaches clearly depend on, and supplement, each other. How the stone hurts my foot or how the sun warms the earth can and must be explained in terms of general laws, even though those laws must be supplemented by reference to a constellation of individual circumstances before they allow specific conclusions. What really distinguishes methods we call nomothetic or ideographic is emphasis on one or the other aspect.

There are essentially two reasons why sociology tends to be ideographic. One is that individual phenomena retain our interest much more in the social than in the physical sciences. Once a generalisation is established or confirmed, the chemist will discard the chemicals on his workbench without further thought; the sociologist will remain interested in the story of 'Middletown' or the origins of Western capitalism. The other reason is that the laws which govern relationships between individuals within society are not sociological laws. We can, for example, explain the universal fact of family life in terms of biological, psychological, and economic laws, but the sociologically interesting features of marriage and family life in a particular society only makes sense in terms of their specific social and cultural contexts. These considerations have made it important to legitimise the ideographic approach by examining it critically, justifying it rationally, and using it systematically. Modern developments in this direction include so-called systems science and various forms of structuralism, which by using organic structures, logical systems, and machines with feedback mechanisms as their models, envisage hierarchies of configurations in which individual things are determined by their place within the configuration.

In this context special mention must be made of hermeneutics, which combines the ideographic approach and explanation in terms of part/whole relationships, with a direct concern for the subjective meaning which human agents impart to social life.[23] The discipline of hermeneutics, which today attracts increasing attention, goes back to the Greeks. It was, originally, the methodology of interpreting texts, and as such played a large part as a theological discipline during the centuries in which doctrinal disagreement made the interpretation of the Bible of paramount importance. Developed and refined over the centuries, it was given a broader meaning and greater theoretical sophistication by Friedrich Schleiermacher in the first, and by Wilhelm Dilthey in the second part of the nineteenth century. By the twentieth century, the ground was prepared for hermeneutics to become an alternative, or more precisely a supplementary, methodology of the social sciences.

Two arguments converge to make the case for sociology as an interpretative, and therefore hermeneutic, discipline. One is that the evidence available to sociologists very largely consists of texts (such as reports, legal documents, or codes of practice) or of oral communication and expressive behaviour. The careful and skilled interpretation of these communications is therefore a substantial part of the sociologist's job. The other argument is that the sociologist, like the literary critic, must be concerned with subjective meaning, because the meaning which individuals attribute to the situations they find themselves in provides the motives for their actions. Hermeneutics is therefore needed to supplement a scientific approach which confines itself to establishing causal connections and general laws.

To correct the deeply entrenched bias in favour of scientific methods, advocates of hermeneutics have emphasised that methods of interpretation have been practiced as long as those of the physical sciences and have been refined over centuries by traditional disciplines such as theology, jurisprudence, literary criticism, and philology. In these disciplines truth matters as much as in science, and is thought to be attainable. Salvation depends on getting the meaning of sacred texts right, life and liberty on the interpretation of the law. It would be unreasonable to reject this tradition wholesale. Instead we need to restore it to its rightful place by justifying and explaining its procedures.

Methodological questions arise wherever knowledge is sought, but if there is an easy solution or if methods have already proved their worth, methodology appears a luxury or even an intrusion. The successful researcher (like the centipede when asked how it coordinated its legs) may be confused by being asked to reflect on his methods. In the case of sociology which continues to face a sceptical world, the case is different. It needs to convince people that it can provide reliable and valuable knowledge. That is why questions about the soundness of its presuppositions and the rigour of its methods require attention.

The Contribution of the Philosophy of Reason

On the social and political scene we have seen in this century that 'the sleep of reason breeds monsters'.[24] In the sphere of scholarship the issue is not quite so dramatic but still evokes serious concern. That is why the concept 'rationality' has reappeared in books and articles about the methodology of the social sciences,[25] and why there has been a good deal of play with the term 'critical' (as in 'critical theory'), which must surely imply rational scrutiny. Against this backcloth of current sociological concerns we can review the contribution which the philosophy of reason can make to contemporary thought.

To appreciate the arguments of the philosophers we examined, it was imperative to see them in their historical setting and philosophic context. Now that we want to assess their contemporary relevance, we must reassemble their conclusions thematically.

On the question whether reason has something to say outside the sphere of science and the application of means to ends, Descartes's contribution is more limited and ambiguous than that of the other philosophers, partly because he considers the problem solved once he has demonstrated the existence of a perfect God who guarantees the truth of painstaking thought, and partly because he takes it for granted that the God of his philosophy is the Christian God and that therefore the teaching of the church provides reliable guidance. Descartes's arguments, apart from being perfunctory on this matter, are also double-edged, for his insistence on a degree of precision and certainty only attainable in mathematics devalues the use of reason in other spheres.

Plato's argument is, in contrast, direct and powerful. In our search for knowledge we have no option but to look beyond the deceptive sphere of appearances towards an ideal world in which our reason is at home. This ideal world contains the norms of perfection and so provides us with guiding principles. The pursuit of knowledge yields moral principles as well, because reason tells us how to act so as to be at one with, or at least closer to, the ultimate reality of which we have only a vague intimation in everyday life.

Spinoza is as speculatively bold as Plato, but for him reason has no need to soar beyond possible experience, because a rational order, though we may grasp it imperfectly, permeates our lives. The more we discover about this order, the better we understand our true interest (towards which we are naturally disposed) and so learn how to organise society justly. Once reason has disclosed the structure of reality, it has also defined our goals; its only remaining task is to dispel stupidity and overcome the power of the passions.

Kant's argument is more complex, difficult, and austerely formal than those of his predecessors but also awe-inspiring in the incisiveness with which it goes to the heart of the issue. For Kant reason steps beyond the theoretical, cognitive sphere by choosing itself as a basis for both knowledge and morality. To be true to your reason is the whole law. The authority which reason thus claims rests in his philosophy on different grounds from those offered by the other philosophers discussed here. Unlike them, he does not believe that reason could know, and find itself at one with, ultimate reality. Instead he considers it at home within empirical reality, of which it is the co-author. From this he concludes that reason, which must be active and autonomous to make sense of an alien reality, can impose its principles of consistency and impartial adherence to rules on our practical activities as well.

The arguments of these four thinkers have, it will be noted, one thing in common. In spite of important differences between them, they all agree that unless reason is capable of operating in a wider sphere than that of scientific knowledge, it cannot even provide a proper basis for that knowledge.

Turning from the general role of reason (and therefore its place in sociology) to its function within human personality, we find that the contributions of our philosophers answer two questions in particular: How is the mind related to the body? and How is reason related to such other mental factors as passions and instincts? Plato's view on the first is clear and, on the whole, unhelpful to modern sociology. For him the body is the valueless shell, or even the prison, of the mind. Only death liberates us from this imprisonment (and because philosophy too frees us from bondage to the material, it is a kind of dying). This view has had the negative effect of encouraging asceticism and scorn of empirical investigations, but it has also encouraged the realisation that pure thought, including mathematical calculation, is important for discovering what the world is like.

Descartes's dualism preserves the commonsense view of the matter and provides a basis for the common practice of sociologists to relate material and cultural or intellectual factors to each other. He fails, however, to give a very illuminating account of the relationship between the two, and his very sharp separation of body from mind has encouraged the cleavage between behaviourists, who deal scientifically with bodily behaviour, and phenomenologists, who introspect mental activities.

Spinoza's psychophysical parallelism ingeniously solves many of the problems which puzzled Descartes and has useful methodological consequences, such as warning us, for example, against mixing up physical and mental explanation. It is flawed by one large difficulty. In some respects the complete parallelism between the operations in the two spheres remains an empty article of faith, because, prima facie, the two spheres are quite differently structured. (What, for example, could correspond in nature to the logical and grammatical rules according to which we arrange our thoughts?)

Kant has relatively little to say about the relation between mind and body, because he draws his essential distinctions along different lines. The mind's states and activities, which we can observe or introspect, are as much part of the empirical world as our bodies and the physical events around us and are subject to the same laws. Only the cognitive 'I' lies outside the empirical world and thus escapes such scrutiny. It is related to the rest of the mind and the outside world as the subject to the object in cognition. The significance of this idea will become clearer when we take up the topic of the sociology of knowledge.

On the relation between reason and other aspects of the mind Kant also diverges sharply from the other three philosophers, who all thought that reason can and should tame, channel, and direct man's various impulses or instincts and thus harmonise the whole personality. For Plato reason is perfectly fitted to adjudicate between different motives and by governing the whole personality achieve the optimal fulfilment not only of reason but of all the mind's constituent parts. Rational control thus provides both happiness and mental health. Descartes is more interested in the theoretical and technical use of reason than in its power to harmonise the personality, and in a way he takes for granted the power of reason to direct action in the light of knowledge. In Spinoza, on the other hand, we find elaborate theories about the way in which reason can get the better of our passions, serve our interest, and put us on the way to happiness.

Thus, though all four thinkers are at one in believing that reason is an essential part of man and that man's highest fulfilment lies in the exercise of reason itself, Plato, Descartes, and Spinoza also share the conviction that reason can promote our happiness and with it social harmony, because a recognition of our true interests involves recognising the need for ordered societies. Kant's view is more pessimistic. The rule of reason either in personal life or in society does not lead necessarily to happiness. On the contrary it may demand suffering and self-sacrifice, because man might be happier if at the expense of others he had more of the world's goods or escaped onerous duties. But reason demands fair shares for all. Most people do not want to pay taxes or serve as soldiers, but is it reasonable to avoid contributing to an organisation on which one's life depends? Being rational is not the same as being prudent, because there is no empirical evidence that we reap any rewards for being rational and moral, and often we have to pay a price for it. Indeed, even in its technical and prudential role reason may not lead us as efficiently as the instincts do other animals.

The functions which the four thinkers attributed to reason are not exclusive, and each provides a useful point of departure for the study of society. Reason as the capacity to choose one's means effectively, reason as harmonising personal and social life, the search for knowledge as an important social goal, and, finally, reason as an independent source of morality are all socialy significant themes. Even Kant's austere moral philosophy, though uncongenial in the contemporary climate of opinion, which favours neither puritanism nor moral ardour, remains relevant if only as a corrective for inadequacies of alternative accounts. Neither self-interest nor social utility explains the often harsh voice of conscience, in response to which people accept trouble and sacrifices. However much we take the long view about balancing social advantages, these considerations do not add up to what morality seems to be about. The sociologist encounters moral imperatives as part of social reality; he has to take account of freedom and responsibility and of unreconciled conflicts within human nature. Do we have a theory which accounts for all these phenomena better than Kant's moral philosophy?

Methodology, our third theme, is as much indebted to the philosophy of reason as is philosophic anthropology, because we can understand much better what is involved in achieving objective and reliable knowledge (which is, obviously, the central aim of methodology) when we look at the contributions of our four philosophers to the questions we have already posed: What is the relation between theory and facts in sociology? What order can we attribute to the human world? and Can the ideographic approach to sociology be rationally justified?

On the question of the importance of theory all four thinkers speak with one voice. Plato argues that observation by itself cannot constitute knowledge because it provides a varied and changing flux of impressions instead of a fixed and definable object. The observer can only understand the flickering shadows of sense experience by relating them to patterns which reason beheld before birth (that is, to innate ideas). The concepts we impose on experience (or at least the more abstract and important ones) are thus not generalisations from common properties but norms for what something, be it a doctor or a society, must be like to deserve the name. From there it is only a step to Plato's theory of ideal types, which has become a familiar concept and a useful tool for sociologists. For Descartes, too, only the judgement of reason transforms the flotsam of sense data into knowledge of objects. When we report seeing a piece of wax, or people passing beneath our window, we are making a judgement, for what we literally see is a yellow patch or dark shapes.[26] Spinoza recognises that the mind is active, but in his case this recognition has a quite specific significance for sociology, because it anticipates the idea of stereotypes. According to Spinoza, when we judge or label things we tend to simplify and even distort them. Kant's contribution, on the other hand, is the thoroughness and penetration with which he analyses the role of reason in the act of cognition. Thus the philosophy of reason provides a massive case in favour of the view that we can only grasp facts within a theoretical framework.

As for our presuppositions about the order we can expect in our subject matter, both Descartes and Spinoza postulate a universal causality. Kant agrees with them about this universality but attributes it to the structuring activity of the mind rather than to reality. Plato, less interested in causality, spells out very fully the idea of a functional order within a purposefully structured universe. Kant echoes this view more tentatively by arguing that it is necessary to adopt a teleological point of view in order to understand living things and works of art.[27] A third structuring principle of social reality, the idea of an objective sphere of mind, is anticipated and developed to various degrees by all four philosophers. In Plato the forms constitute this objective sphere, which individual minds remember and reach out to. For Descartes individual minds are merely part of mind, which is one of the two substances constituting reality. In Spinoza the minds of individuals are, similarly, parts of a single mind, which in his case is one aspect of a single substance. To Kant the mind which structures experience is not merely the mind of a particular individual but something we all share.

To these assumptions about a causal, functional, and mind-imposed order we must add Spinoza's idea that reality is an individual consisting of individuals, a system of hierarchically arranged systems, an infinitely complex and intricate structure resembling an enormously varied and finely attuned organism.

The assumptions we have listed can be easily translated into methodological recommendations such as 'use causal explanations' or 'analyse structure in terms of the relationships between wholes and parts'. To them we can add Descartes's methodological principle which requires that any subject should be analysed into its component elements and explained in terms of them. Though originally designed for, and found effective in, the physical sciences, this principle has its place in the social ones.

The question of hermeneutics is in a different category, because it concerns the respectability of sociology. Being ideographic and about meaning, hermeneutics makes a sociology which uses it very different from a science. On this topic Spinoza made a crucial contribution by arguing powerfully that the study of individuals and their relations to each other puts us on the way to an essential and, indeed, the highest form of knowledge.

'Causality', 'system', 'function', and 'ideal type' have their secure place in sociological theory, and such methods as mathematical analysis and hermeneutic interpretation are widely used in sociology. It is a testimony to their viability and fruitfulness that they have been successfully used without reference to, let alone acceptance of, the philosophical contexts in which they were originally developed and justified. Critical examination of these sources may, however, make them into even more powerful tools and help us to understand even better what we are doing with them.

Epistemology and the Sociology of Knowledge

By turning, for a moment, to the sociology of knowledge we can most pointedly focus attention on the questions we have been discussing. In other branches of sociology, say industrial sociology, we can dodge a discussion of the scope and limits of sociology, because the sociologist's own approach is not directly at issue when he studies relations between workers and management. But when knowledge is the subject, the sociologist's own cognitive processes are under scrutiny too. This problem

of self-examination raises a hornets' nest of methodological issues. In fact the general problem of a methodology of sociology
is raised here in its sharpest form, and once we begin examining
our cognitive processes and the extent to which self-knowledge
is possible, we have also broached the theme of human nature.
Finally, these radical questions carry us to the frontiers of sociology and make its relationship to philosophy visible.

The sociology of knowledge as an independent discipline,
pioneered by Max Scheler, powerfully promoted by Karl Mannheim, and currently refined by sociologists like Peter Berger and
Thomas Luckman, is a relatively recent growth, but the idea that
cognitive processes are rooted in social activities, and use socially
conditioned tools, has been an integral part of sociology from
the start.[28] Indeed, we have seen the idea taking shape in the
philosophy of reason. In his theory of education Plato recognises
explicitly the role which family background, music, games, stories, and physical exercises play in shaping the outlook, thinking, and cognitive capacity of children; and when he explains
how a corrupt society corrupts philosophic natures, he makes
it clear how social norms discourage or encourage scholarship.
The same point is made even more powerfully in his metaphor
of the prisoners in the cave, for the bondage from which they
need freeing is clearly social conditioning, and turning them
round from looking at shadows to a contemplation of true
reality,[29] a reconditioning. Descartes sketches, though in a rather
casual, throwaway manner, the outlines of a sociology of knowledge, when he remarks that circumstances, such as 'good fortune', the civilisation we are born in, and even our health and
temperament, may determine what we believe to be true, what
methods we adopt (and therefore how successful we are) in our
search for knowledge, and how far we are willing to depart from
well-trodden paths. Spinoza contributes to the sociology of
knowledge by making two related points, namely that the pursuit of knowledge is an important social goal and that it depends
on the existence of a reasonably stable social order. Kant's contribution is more substantial than those of the others, because
it goes beyond the relatively obvious fact about the relevance of
social conditions, to the heart of the matter, namely how such
conditioning is logically possible. His idea that the mind actively

imposes its own principles of order on the world of experience is a vital link in making the 'social construction of reality'[30] intelligible.

The sociology of knowledge is noncontroversial and epistemologically harmless where it stops short of the question of truth. Cooperation between several—and sometimes many—people, the creation of institutions, and the provision of material resources is undoubtedly needed for most, if not all, research and it can therefore be fruitful to study how the presence or absence of these factors and their efficient or inefficient functioning affects the success of various branches of knowledge, or even of particular research projects. The availability of these different resources is itself socially conditioned (for example by public indifference to the subject), and this too can be studied. The sociology of knowledge can, however, remain unproblematical only as long as it can take for granted a clear distinction between knowledge and beliefs and confine its activities to the former while leaving the latter to a sociology of belief, which could investigate the social reasons why people believe something, for in the case of knowledge the grounds we have for believing it, are rational not social. The study of ideologies, which has loomed large in Marxist sociology, is part of such a sociology of belief. The gist of this approach is to show—as it has often done successfully—that people hold a particular belief because it serves their interest (by, for example, justifying an arrangement which is to their advantage).

The question is, however, whether the sociologist can, from his point of view, really distinguish knowledge from belief. Social forces are at work affecting all of us and colouring all our attitudes and thoughts. What counts as good evidence and so establishes knowledge is itself a subject of social consensus and may well, as some sociologists have argued, be conditioned by the interest of a group or class. By pushing this line of inquiry consistently and quite properly to its limits, the sociologist appears to cut off the branch on which he sits. If the theory that someone's belief is an ideology is itself nothing but someone else's (in this case the sociologist's) ideology, it can be of little value or interest. Sociology must produce knowledge not ideologies; so we are back with the question how we can establish independently what constitutes knowledge. Berger and Luckman have made this point very lucidly: 'Mannheim's readiness to include epistemological questions concerning the validity of sociological knowledge in the sociology of knowledge is somewhat like trying to push a bus in which one is riding.'[31]

This paradoxical situation, that sociology cannot pursue its subject to the limits without putting its own standing in question, can only be disentangled by showing that it is not a problem soluble within a single discipline. The case of the sociology of knowledge is so instructive because it brings home to us that we can only gain knowledge and appreciate it for what it is in a wider context of which philosophy forms a part.

The fact is that sociology and philosophy overlap very largely in their subject matter, which is man's life and activities, even though the one emphasises the social, the other the intellectual and theoretical, aspects of the subject. That is why we have a philosophy as well as a sociology of religion, art, law, and knowledge. For that matter we have both a philosophy of sociology and a sociology of philosophy. The sociological and philosophical approaches are highly relevant to each other but must never be merged or muddled if we are to avoid intellectual chaos. It is the nature of their approach which distinguishes them, and one reason for presenting the ideas of various philosophers in their context was to illustrate *how* the philosophical approach differed from that of sociology.

By clarifying the concept of knowledge, philosophy not only secures the foundations of the sociology of knowledge but also throws light on its subject matter. Claims that social factors, such as economic interests, the structure of society, or class membership affect thought abound in the literature of the sociology of knowledge, but explanations as to precisely how this takes place are not as abundant. Lucien Goldmann, for example, has argued that because economic activity is essential to provide for the needs of men, it 'has always been of capital importance as regards their way of thinking.'[32] The premise is impeccable, and so would be the conclusion if it meant no more than that people *think* that economic factors are important. But the 'way of thinking' surely suggests more, and what this could be is not so clear. Could it be that we do our sums differently or draw different conclusions from the same premises according to our economic interests? Or if not, what are the subtle ways in which our thoughts about the world are affected? Only a very searching epistemological analysis of what is involved in cognition can provide the framework for showing how cognition is or can be socially affected. Without this careful analysis, vague intimations, like Marx's, that 'social existence determines consciousness',[33] sound too much like ideology themselves.

These questions about the sociology of knowledge, like the more general ones about reason, human nature, and methodology, cannot be settled once and for all. Continuing the debate on these matters is important, though, because that alone can show what is required to get nearer to the answers. No subject, certainly not sociology, can be the sole judge in its own case. In its search for secure foundations and rigorous methods sociology can profit from philosophy, as it also can from other disciplines, be it mathematics or psychology. Philosophy, certainly, can look back on a tradition of ideas which can still help to make sociological debate more precise and meaningful.

Notes

The main purpose of these notes, particularly those to chapters 2–5, is to provide cross-references to the texts on which each chapter is based. These references are as complete and precise as possible so as to help the reader to check my assertions and study the texts themselves. Other references are intended to illustrate rather than to document fully the range of relevant literature.

Chapter 1

1. See H. R. Trevor-Roper's *The European Witchcraze of the 16th and 17th Centuries* (Harmondsworth: Penguin, 1969), pp. 109-11.

2. *Dialogues of Plato*, trans. Benjamin Jowett, ed. J. D. Kaplan (New York: Pocket Library, 1951), pp. 10-11.

3. K. R. Popper, *The Logic of Scientific Discovery* (London: Hutchinson, 1972).

4. This is a paraphrase of John Stuart Mill's assertion that "it is better to be a human being dissatisfied than a pig satisfied, better to be Socrates dissatisfied than a fool satisfied." *Utilitarianism* (London: Dent/Everyman's Library, 1918), p. 9.

5. See August Comte, *The Positive Philosophy*, trans. Harriet Martineau, 2 vols. (London: Chapman, 1853).

6. See, for example, R. A. Nisbett, *The Sociological Tradition* (London: Heinemann, 1967).

7. See, for instance, Max Weber, 'Objectivity in Social Science and Social Policy', and Leo Strauss, 'Natural Right and the Distinction between Facts and Values', both reproduced in *Philosophy of the Social Sciences*, ed. Maurice Nathanson (New York: Random House, 1963). See also Max Weber, 'Science as a Vocation', in *From Max Weber*, ed.

154

H. H. Gerth and C. Wright Mills (London: Routledge & Kegan Paul, 1970); and R. S. Lynd, *Knowledge for What?* (Princeton: Princeton University Press, 1939).

Chapter 2

1. This charge was pressed most vigorously by K. R. Popper, *The Open Society and Its Enemies*, vol. 1 (London: Routledge & Kegan Paul, 1945).

2. The first set of numbers given in my references to the *Republic* (R) are the standard references to the Oxford edition, which pinpoint passages from any translation. The second set of figures (P) give the pages of the translation I have used, the Penguin Classic version by Desmond Lee (Harmondsworth, 1955). R331–36, P55–62.

3. R338, P65.
4. R338, P66.
5. R339, P67.
6. R340, P68.
7. R343, P72.
8. R343, P73.
9. R351, P82.
10. R346–47, P75.
11. R578–80, P351–54.
12. R549, P319.
13. R556, P328.
14. R577, P351.
15. R342–43, P69–70.
16. R342, P71.
17. R352–53, P84–85.
18. R353, P85.
19. R352, P84.
20. R505–9, P268–73.
21. R509, P273.
22. R352–53, P84–85.
23. R597, 601, P373, 378.
24. R588–89, P365–66, where Plato suggests that reason is the man-like in man.
25. R476–79, P238–43.
26. While goodness is discussed in the already mentioned section on the Good, truth is referred to in terms of the approach to knowledge presented in the analogies of the line and the cave. R509–19, P276–84. Beauty is discussed in the *Symposium*; see particularly pp. 216–17 in

Jowett's translation in *Dialogues of Plato*, ed. J. D. Kaplan (New York: Popular Library, 1951).

27. R433–34, P182.

28. R592, P369.

29. R545–92, P315–69.

30. Émile Durkheim, *Selected Writings*, ed. Anthony Giddens (Cambridge: Cambridge University Press, 1972), pp. 42, 173–82.

31. Max Weber, *The Methodology of the Social Sciences*, ed. E. A. Shils and H. A. Finch (Chicago: Free Press, 1949), pp. 89–105.

32. R585, P360–61.

33. R571–72, P344–45.

34. This line of argument is implied throughout rather than specifically stated; but see R353–389, P85–166, 195, as well as the section on the Good.

35. R582, P356.

36. R442–44, P194–97.

37. R358–59, P89–90.

38. R369–71, P102–5.

39. R368, P101.

40. R368, P101–2.

41. R428–29, P175–76.

42. R375–76, P111.

43. R499, P261.

44. R518, P283.

45. R376–402, P114–42.

46. R549–50, 553, 559–60, P320–21, 324–25, 332–33.

47. R572–73, P345–46.

48. R490–93, P252–55.

49. R457–61, P212–18.

50. R416–20, P162–64.

Chapter 3

1. Giordano Bruno, Italian philosopher of the Renaissance, burned at the stake by the Inquisition in 1600.

2. In 1633.

3. All my references are to page numbers in *Discourse on Method*, trans. Arthur Wollaston (Harmondsworth: Penguin, 1960); the book includes the *Meditations*. Pages 40–42.

4. He actually criticises the state of logic, algebra, and geometry but encourages and envisages a judicious combination of the three, p. 49.

5. 50.

6. 51.

7. 60–61.

8. 106.

9. For instance, 119.

10. 61, 108.

11. 110–11.

12. 120–21.

13. 62.

14. 123.

15. 147.

16. 139.

17. 158–66.

18. H. R. Trevor-Roper, *The European Witchcraze of the 16th and 17th Centuries* (Harmondsworth: Penguin, 1969).

19. Dilip Hiron, 'The Coloured View of the British', *New Society*, 22 February 1968, pp. 261–66.

20. See R. A. Nisbett, *The Sociological Tradition* (London: Heinemann, 1967).

21. Gilbert Ryle, *The Concept of Mind* (New York: Barnes & Noble, 1960).

22. By Ryle, pp. 15–16, who thought that it fitted Descartes's view. Indeed he describes it as Descartes's myth.

23. 109.

24. 86.

25. 42–43.

26. 84. This is the passage which made me call Descartes a prophet of technology.

27. 36.

28. 41.

29. 42.

30. 37.

31. 36.

32. 85.

33. 37–38.

34. 40.

35. 43.

36. 53.

37. 42–43, referred to above in note 24.

Chapter 4

1. In Spinoza's *Ethic* the easiest and clearest references are to the numbers of the propositions, definitions, etc., that subdivide the larger Parts (roman numerals) of the work. Part IV, App. 13.

2. IV, App. 17.

3. My discussion of Spinoza's concept of God is largely based on Part I, called 'On God'. As this is not very long and the definitions, axioms, propositions, and notes are closely knit together, I have in this case not referred to individual propositions.

4. In Part II.

5. II, Prop. 21.

6. This issue is largely dealt with in Part II.

7. I, Axiom III, Prop. 33; also IV, Def. 3.

8. I, Def. VII.

9. See Max Weber, *The Methodology of the Social Sciences*, ed. E. A. Shils and H. A. Finch (Chicago: Free Press, 1949), pp. 124–25.

10. II, Prop. 40.

11. II, Lemma VII Note.

12. II, Def. VII.

13. A debate on this subject has been assembled in *Modes of Individualism and Collectivism*, ed. J. O. Neill (London: Heinemann, 1973).

14. II, Prop. 6.

15. II, Prop. 13.

16. III, Prop. 2.

17. II, Prop. 7; V, Prop. 1.

18. III, Props. 6–9.

19. III, Prop 11.

20. III, Prop. 13.

21. III, Introduction.

22. II, Def. VI; IV, Preface.

23. IV, Preface, Defs. I, II.

24. IV, Prop, 19.

25. IV, Prop. 37 Note 2.

26. IV, Prop. 26.

27. IV, Props. 32, 34, 35, 36, 37.

28. IV, Props. 40, 73.

29. IV, App. 13, 14.

30. IV, Prop. 45 Note.

31. IV, Props. 3, 4.

32. IV, Props. 5, 6, 7.

33. V, Props. 3, 4.

34. V, Prop. 40.

35. IV, Prop. 59.

36. IV, Prop. 61.

37. V, Prop. 20.

38. V, Props. 15, 16.

39. II, Prop. 16.

40. II, Prop. 17.

41. II, Props. 22, 23, 24, 25, 27, 28, 29.

42. II, Prop. 40 Note 2.

43. II, Props. 35, 42.

44. II, Props. 38, 39, 40.

45. II, Prop. 40 Note 2.

46. See, for example, G. A. Lundberg, *Foundations of Sociology* (New York: McKay, 1939); Otto Neurath, 'Sociology and Physialism', in *Logical Positivism*, ed. Alfred Ayer (London: Allen & Unwin, 1959); and Richard von Mises, *Positivism* (New York: Dover Publications, 1968). See also K. R. Popper, *The Poverty of Historicism* (London: Routledge & Kegan Paul, 1957), pp. 130–43.

47. See, for instance, Maurice Nathanson, *Phenomenology, Role and Reason* (Springfield, Ill.: C. C. Thomas, 1974); Alfred Schutz, *Collected Papers*, 3 vols. (The Hague: Nijhoff, 1964-67); and also Jürgen Habermas, *Knowledge and Human Interests* (Boston: Beacon Press, 1971).

48. I, App. 10.

49. This is Hegel's phrase; see *Lectures on the Philosophy of History* (New York: The Willey Book Co., 1944), p. 16.

50. See Wilhelm Dilthey, 'The Development of Hermeneutics', in *Wilhelm Dilthey: Selected Writings*, ed. H. P. Rickman (Cambridge: Cambridge University Press, 1976); and R. E. Palmer, *Hermeneutics* (Evanston, Ill.: Northwestern University Press, 1969).

51. See, for example, *From Max Weber*, ed. H. H. Gerth and C. Wright Mills (London: Routledge & Kegan Paul, 1970), pp. 240–44.

52. I have already referred to the discussion in Neill, *Modes of Individualism and Collectivism* (note 13 above).

Chapter 5

All references to the *Critique of Pure Reason* are given in terms of the pagination of the original first (A) and second (B) editions. To these I have added the pages references to the English translation (K) by N. Kemp-Smith (London: Macmillan, 1933). Bxvi–xvii, K22.

2. B44–45, 69, A250, K72–74, 88, 268.

3. B116–25, K120–26.

4. Max Herkheimer, *Critical Theory*, trans. M. Y. O'Connell and others (New York: Hessler and Hessler, 1972), p. 208.

5. B180, K183.

6. B33–34, K65–66.

7. B37–73, K67–91.

8. B129–30, K151–52.

9. B131–38, K152–57.

10. B195, K193.

11. B197, K194.

12. B75, K93.

13. B104, K112.

14. B232–48, K218–28.

15. The first set of figures referring to Kant's *Groundwork of the Metaphysics of Morals* is to the second edition (G); the second set (P) refers to H. J. Paton's translation in *The Moral Law* (London: Hutchinson University Library, 1978). G20–21, P68–69.

16. G1–4, P59–60.

17. G13, P65.

18. G3, P60.

19. G1, 13, P59, 65.

20. G10–11, P63–64.

21. G14–15, P65–66.

22. G28–29, P73–74.

23. G29, P73.

24. G36, P76.

25. G17, P67.

26. G52, P84.

27. This illustration is mine, but Kant gives similar ones, G53–57, P84–86.

28. G37, P78.

29. G7, P62.

30. G8–10, P63–64.

31. G39–48, P78–83.

32. G127–28, P123.

33. G20, P68.

34. G77–79, P96–97.

35. Giii–vii, P54–55.

36. G126, P122.

37. G83, P97.

38. For the former view see, for instance, B. L. Whorf, *Language, Thought and Reality* (Cambridge, Mass.: MIT Press, 1967). For the latter view, see Noam Comsky, *Language and Mind* (New York: Harcourt Brace, 1972).

39. See, for example, Ernst Cassierer, *The Philosophy of Symbolic Forms* (New Haven: Yale University Press, 1953).

40. G97–99, P107–8.

41. G105–10, P111–13.

42. See G. H. Mead, *Mind, Self and Society* (Chicago, 1934).

Chapter 6

1. See H. Marcuse on Husserl, 'On Science and Phenomenology', in *Positivism and Sociology*, ed. Anthony Giddens (London: Heinemann, 1974).

2. Edward Shils, 'The Calling of Sociology', in *Themes of Society*, Talcot Parsons et al (New York: Free Press, 1965), pp. 1417–18. T. Burns, 'The Study of Industry', in *Society, Problems, and Methods of Study*, ed. A. T. Welford, Michael Argyle, D. V. Glass, Y. N. Morris (London: Routledge & Kegan Paul, 1962), p. 214.

3. See, for instance, Max Weber, 'Objectivity in Social Science and Social Policy', and Leo Strauss, 'Natural Right and the Distinction between Facts and Values', both reproduced in *Philosophy of the Social Sciences*, ed. Maurice Nathanson (New York: Random House, 1963).

4. *New Society*, 11 February 1971, p. 406.

5. Max Weber, *The Methodology of the Social Sciences*, ed. E. A. Shils and H. A. Finch (Chicago: Free Press, 1949), p. 76.

6. See, for example, Max Scheler, 'Man and History', in *Philosophical Perspectives*, trans. O. A. Haac (Boston: Beacon Press, 1958); Ernst Cassierer, *An Essay on Man* (New Haven: Yale University Press, 1944); and Helmuth Plessner, *Die Stufen des Organischen und der Mensch* (Berlin: Gruyter, 1928).

7. Quoted in I. C. Jarvie, *Concepts and Society* (London: Routledge & Kegan Paul, 1972), p. 134.

8. D. H. Wrong, 'The Oversocialised Conception of Man in Modern Sociology', in *Humanistic Society*, ed. J. G. Glass and J. R. Staude (Pacific Palisades, Calif.: Good Year, 1972), p. 71.

9. One may think, for example, of the challenge to older views about the immutability and uniformity of human nature, that came from the work of Margaret Mead, for instance in *Male and Female* (Westport, Ct.: Greenwood Press, 1977).

10. R343–44, P72–73 (see chapter 2 above for source abbreviations).

11. R358–59, P89–90.

12. The phrase is David Hume's, *A Treatise of Human Nature* (London: Everyman's Library, 1966), Vol. II, p. 127.

13. The debate reproduced in *The Positivist Dispute in German Sociology*, ed. Glyn Adey (London: Heinemann, 1976), is an illustration of this ongoing discussion.

14. Auguste Comte, *The Positive Philosophy*, trans. Harriet Martineau, 2 vols. (London: Chapman, 1853), 2:242.

15. Erving Goffmann, *Behaviour in Public Places* (Glencoe, Ill.: The Free Press, 1963), p. 4.

16. Gunnar Myrdal, *Objectivity in Social Research* (London: Routledge & Kegan Paul, 1972).

17. In a review of *Causation and Functionalism in Sociology*, by W. W. Isajiw, *New Society*, 7 March 1968, p. 354.

18. K. R. Popper, 'On the Theory of Objective Mind', in *Objective Knowledge* (Oxford: Oxford University Press, 1972).

19. Émile Durkheim, *The Elementary Forms of Religious Life*, trans. Y, W. Swain, (London: G. Allen & Unwin, 1946), p. 437.

20. See Heinrich Rickert, *Kulturwissenschaft und Naturwissenschaft* (Freiburg: J. C. B. Mohr, 1899).

21. John Madge, quoted in *The Listener*, 27 June 1963, p. 1067.

22. Lucien Goldmann, *The Human Sciences and Philosophy* (London: Jonathan Cape, 1969), p. 86.

23. See Wilhelm Dilthey, 'The Development of Hermeneutics', in *Wilhelm Dilthey: Selected Writings*, ed. H. P. Rickman (Cambridge: Cambridge University Press, 1976); and R. E. Palmer, *Hermeneutics* (Evanston, Ill.: Northwestern University Press, 1969).

24. A caption to one of Goya's drawings.

25. For example, Jonathan Bennet, *Rationality* (New York: Routledge & Kegan Paul, 1964); S. I. Benn and G. W. Mortimore, eds., *Rationality and the Social Sciences* (London: Routledge & Kegan Paul, 1976); Alfred Schutz, 'The Problems of Rationality in the Social World', in *Collected Papers*, vol. 2 (The Hague: Nijhoff, 1964); and B. R. Wilson, ed., *Rationality* (Oxford: Basil Blackwell, 1970).

26. *Discourse on Method*, pp. 114–16 (see chapter 3 above for edition).

27. Immanuel Kant, *The Critique of Judgement*, trans. H. Bernard (New York: Macmillan, 1974).

28. Max Scheler, *Problems of a Sociology of Knowledge*, trans. M. S. Frings (London: Routledge & Kegan Paul, 1980); Karl Mannheim, *Ideology and Utopia* (London: Routledge & Kegan Paul, 1960); Mannheim, *Essays on the Sociology of Knowledge* (London: Routledge & Kegan Paul, 1952); and Werner Stark, *The Sociology of Knowledge* (New York: Free Press, 1958).

29. Plato, *The Republic*, trans. Desmond Lee (Harmondsworth: Penguin, 1955), pp. 278–86.

30. This is the title of P. L. Berger's and Thomas Luckmann's, *The Social Construction of Reality* (London: A. Cawe, 1966).

31. Quoted in Jarvie, *Concepts and Society*, p. 136.

32. Lucien Goldmann, *The Human Sciences and Philosophy*, p. 87.

33. Karl Marx, *Contributions to the Critique of Political Economy* (London: Lawrence & Wisharst, 1971).

Bibliography

Texts

Descartes, Réné. *Discourse on Method*. Translated by Arthur Wollaston. Harmondsworth: Penguin, 1960.

Kant, Immanuel, *The Critique of Pure Reason*. Translated by Norman Kemp–Smith. London: Macmillan, 1933.

————. *Groundwork of the Metaphysic of Morals*. In *The Moral Law*. Edited by H. J. Paton. London: Hutchinson University Library, 1948.

Plato. *Dialogues*. Translated by Benjamin Jowett. Edited by J. C. Kaplan. New York: Pocket Library, 1951.

————. *Republic*. Translated by Desmond Lee. Harmondsworth: Penguin, 1955.

Spinoza, B. *Ethic*. In *Spinoza Selections*. Edited by John Wild. New York: Charles Scribner's Sons, 1930.

Relevant Literature

Adey, Glyn, ed. *The Positivist Dispute in German Sociology*. London: Heinemann, 1976.

Andreski, Stanislav. *Social Sciences as Sorcery*. London: Deutsch, 1972.

Antoni, Carlo. *From History to Sociology*. Detroit: Wayne State University Press, 1950.

Ayer, Alfred, ed. *Logical Positivism*. London: Allen & Unwin, 1959.

Barnes, H. E., and Howard Becker. *Social Thought from Lore to Science*. New York: Dover Publications, 1961.

Beehler, Roger, and A. R. Drengson, eds. *The Philosophy of Society*. London: Methuen, 1978.

Bendix, Reinhard. *Social Science and the Distrust of Reason*. Berkeley and
    Los Angeles: University of California Press, 1951.
Benn, S. I., and G. W. Mortimore, eds. *Rationality and the Social Sciences*.
    London: Routledge & Kegan Paul, 1976.
Bennet, Jonathan. *Rationality*. London: Routledge & Kegan Paul, 1964.
Benton, John. *Philosophic Foundations of the Three Sociologies*. London:
    Routledge & Kegan Paul, 1977.
Berger, P. L. *Invitation to Sociology*. Harmondsworth: Penguin, 1963.
────, and Thomas Luckmann. *The Social Construction of Reality*. Lon-
    don: A. Cawe, 1966.
Bhaskar, Roy. *The Possibility of Naturalism*. Brighton: Harvester Press,
    1979.
Boas, George. *The Limits of Reason*. New York: Greenwood Press, 1961.
Braybrook, Daniel, ed. *Philosophic Problems of the Social Sciences*. New
    York: Macmillan, 1965.
Broadbeck, May, ed. *Readings in the Philosophy of the Social Sciences*.
    Brighton: Harvester Press, 1971.
Brown, S. C., ed. *The Philosophical Disputes in the Social Sciences*. Brighton:
    Harvester Press, 1979.
Brown, Robert. *Explanation in Social Science*. London: Routledge & Kegan
    Paul, 1963.
Cassierer, Ernst. *An Essay on Man*. New Haven: Yale University Press,
    1942.
────. *The Philosophy of Symbolic Forms*. New Haven: Yale University
    Press, 1953.
Chomsky, Noam. *Language and Mind*. New York: Harcourt Brace, 1972.
Comte, Auguste. *The Positive Philosophy*. Translated by Harriet Marti-
    neau. 2 vols. London: Chapman, 1853.
Dahrendorf, Ralf. *Essays in the Theory of Society*. London: Routledge &
    Kegan Paul, 1968.
Dilthey, Wilhelm. *Pattern and Meaning in History*. Edited by H. P. Rick-
    man. New York: Harper, 1962.
────. *Wilhelm Dilthey, Selected Writings*. Edited by H. P. Rickman.
    Cambridge: Cambridge University Press, 1976.
Durkheim, Émile. *The Elementary Form of Religious Life*, vol. 1. Glencoe,
    Ill.: Free Press, 1954.
────. *The Rules of Sociological Method*. New York: Free Press, 1964.
────. *Selected Writings*. Edited by Anthony Giddens. Cambridge:
    Cambridge University Press, 1972.
Emmet, Dorothy, and Alastair MacIntyre, eds. *Sociological Theory and
    Philosophic Analysis*. London: Macmillan, 1970.
Fletcher, Ronald. *The Making of Society*. London: Nelson, 1972.

Garfinkel, Alan. *Forms of Explanation*. New Haven: Yale University Press, 1981.

Gellner, Ernst. *Cause and Meaning in the Social Sciences*. Routledge & Kegan Paul, 1973.

Giddens, Anthony, ed. *Positivism and Sociology*. London: Heinemann, 1974.

Glass, J. G., and J. R. Staude. *Humanistic Society*. Pacific Palisades,: Good Year, 1972.

Goldmann, Lucien. *The Human Sciences and Philosophy*. London: Jonathan Cape, 1969.

Gouldner, W. S. *Enter Plato*. London: Routledge & Kegan Paul, 1967.

Habermas, Jürgen. *Knowledge and Human Interest*. Boston: Beacon Press, 1971.

Hayek, F. A. *The Counter-Revolution of Science*. New York: Free Pres, 1952.

————. *Studies in Philosophy, Politics and Economics*. London: Routledge & Kegan Paul, 1967.

Hegel, G. W. F. *Lectures on the Philosophy of History*, translated by John Sibree. New York: The Willey Books, 1944.

Hindess, Barry. *Philosophy and Methodology in the Social Sciences*. Brighton: Harvester Press, 1977.

Hookway, Christopher, and Philip Pettit, eds. *Action and Interpretation*. Cambridge: Cambridge University Press, 1978.

Hughes, H. S. *Consciousness and Society*. New York: Alfred A. Knopf, 1958.

Isajiw, W. W. *Causation and Functionalism in Sociology*. London: Routledge & Kegan Paul, 1968.

Jarvie, I. C. *Concepts and Society*. London: Routledge & Kegan Paul, 1972.

Kant, Immanuel. *The Critique of Judgement*. Translated by J. H. Bernard. New York: Macmillan, 1974.

Laslett, Peter, and W. G. Runciman, eds. *Philosophy, Politics and Society*. Oxford: Basil Blackwell, 1962.

Levison, A. B. *Knowledge and Society*. New York: Bobbs-Merrill, 1974.

Lukes, Stephen. *Essays in Social Theory*. London: Macmillan, 1977.

Lundberg, G. A. *Foundations of Sociology*. New York: McKay, 1939.

Lynd, R. S. *Knowledge for What?* Princeton: Princeton University Press, 1939.

Mannheim, Karl. *Essays on the Sociology of Knowledge*. London: 1952.

————. *Ideology and Utopia*. London: Routledge & Kegan Paul, 1960.

Marcuse, Herbert. 'On Science and Phenomenology'. In Giddens, *Positivism and Sociology*.

Mead, G. H. *Mind, Self and Society* (Chicago: University of Chicago Press, 1934).

Mead, Margaret. *Male and Female*. Westport, Ct.: Greenwood Press, 1977.

Mill, J. S. Utilitarianism. London: Dent (Everyman's Library), 1918.

Mills, C. Wright. *The Sociological Imagination*. New York: Oxford University Press, 1959.

Mises, Richard von. *Positivism*. New York: Dover Publications, 1969.

———. *Value in Social Theory*. New York: Harper, 1958.

Myrdal, Gunnar. *Objectivity in Social Research*. London: Routledge & Kegan Paul, 1972.

Nagel, Ernest. *The Structure of Science*. New York: Harcourt, Brace & World, 1961.

Nathanson, Maurice. *Phenomenology, Role and Reason*. Springfield, Ill.: C. C. Thomas, 1974.

———, ed. *Philosophy of the Social Sciences*. New York: Random House, 1963.

Nisbett, R. A. *The Sociological Tradition*. London: Heinemann, 1967.

O'Neill, John. *Modes of Individualism and Collectivism*. London: Heinemann, 1973.

Palmer, R.-E. *Hermeneutics*. Evanston, Ill.: Northwestern University Press, 1969.

Plessner, Helmuth. *Die Stufen des Organischen und der Mensch*. Berlin: Gruyter, 1928.

Popper, K. R. *The Logic of Scientific Discovery*. London: Hutchinson, 1977.

———. *Objective Knowledge*. Oxford: Oxford University Press, 1972.

———. *The Open Society and Its Enemies*. London: Routledge & Kegan Paul, 1945.

———. *The Poverty of Historicism*. London: Routledge & Kegan Paul, 1957.

Rex, John. *Key Problems of Sociological Theory*. New York: Humanities Press, 1962.

Rickert, Heinrich. *Kulturwissenschaft und Naturwissenschaft*. Freiburg: J.C.B. Mohr, 1899.

Rickman, H. P. *Understanding and the Human Studies*. London: Heinemann, 1967.

Roche, Maurice. *Phenomenology, Language and the Social Sciences*. London: Routledge & Kegan Paul, 1973.

Rudner, R. S. *Philosophy of Social Science*. Englewood Cliffs, N. J.: Prentice-Hall, 1966.

Runciman, W. G. *Social Science and Political Theory*. Cambridge: Cambridge University Press, 1965.

Ryan, Alan. *The Philosophy of the Social Sciences.* London: Macmillan, 1970.

————, ed. *Philosophy of Social Explanation.* Oxford: Oxford University Press, 1973.

Ryle, Gilbert. *The Concept of Mind.* London: Hutchinson, 1949.

Scheler, Max. *Philosophical Perspectives.* Translated by O. A. Haac. Boston: Beacon Press, 1958.

————. *Problems of a Sociology of Knowledge.* Translated by M. S. Frings. London: Routledge & Kegan Paul, 1980.

Schutz, Alfred. *Collected Papers.* 3 vols. The Hague: Nijhoff, 1964–67.

Stark, Werner. *The Sociology of Knowledge.* New York: Free Press, 1958.

Strauss, Leo. 'Natural Right and the Distinction between Facts and Values'. In Nathanson, *Philosophy of the Social Sciences.*

Timascheff, N. S. *Sociological Theory.* New York: Doubleday, 1955.

Trevor-Roper, H. R. *The European Witchcraze of the 16th and 17th Centuries.* Harmondsworth: Penguin, 1969.

Weber, Max. *From Max Weber.* Edited by H. H. Gerth and C. Wright Mills. London: Routledge & Kegan Paul, 1970.

————. *The Methodology of the Social Sciences.* Edited by E. A. Shils and H. A. Finch. Chicago: Free Press, 1949.

————. 'Objectivity in Social Science and Social Policy'. In Nathanson, *Philosophy of the Social Sciences.*

————. 'Science as a Vocation'. In *From Max Weber.*

————. *The Theory of Social and Economic Organisation.* New York: Free Press, 1964.

Welford, A. T., Michael Argyle, D. V. Glass, and Y. N. Morris. *Society: Problems and Methods of Study.* London: Routledge & Kegan Paul, 1962.

Wilson, B. R., ed. *Rationality.* Oxford: Basil Blackwell, 1970.

Wrong, D. H. 'The Oversocialised Conception of Man in Modern Sociology'. In Glass and Staude, *Humanistic Society.*

Znanietski, Florian. *The Method of Sociology.* New York: Farrar & Rinehart, 1934.

. Index

About the Author

H. P. RICKMAN is Visiting Professor in Philosophy at the City University, London, England. He has written *Meaning in History, Preface to Philosophy, Living with Technology, Understanding and the Human Studies,* and two books on W. Dilthey. His articles have appeared in *The Hibbert Journal International Review of Education, Encyclopedia of Philosophy, Journal of World History,* and *Sociological Analysis,* among others.